All will be well

With this simple guide, it is possible for anyone to follow the Way of the Tao in order to find profound balance and serenity. For thousands of years, the Way has allowed people to:

- unite mind, body, and spirit
- achieve the integration of self
- enjoy a long and healthy life
- have an awareness of our place in the universe
- appreciate the wonder and beauty of nature

Discover a practice of self-cultivation that can reverse bad habits and establish a better way of living—it can be found.

Mark Forstater is the author of *Yoga Masters*, the first book in the Living Wisdom series (available from Plume), as well as several books on spirituality and philosophy. An American producer with over twenty-five years of experience in film and television, he currently lives in London.

THE LIVING WISDOM SERIES

THE TAO

Finding the Way of
Balance and Harmony

Mark Forstater

A PLUME BOOK

To all my daughters—Maya, Asha, Cleo

PLUME
Published by the Penguin Group
Penguin Group (USA) Inc., 375 Hudson Street, New York, New York 10014, U.S.A.
Penguin Group (Canada), 90 Eglinton Avenue East, Suite 700, Toronto, Ontario,
Canada M4P 2Y3 (a division of Pearson Penguin Canada Inc.)
Penguin Books Ltd., 80 Strand, London WC2R 0RL, England
Penguin Ireland, 25 St. Stephen's Green, Dublin 2, Ireland
(a division of Penguin Books Ltd.)
Penguin Group (Australia), 250 Camberwell Road, Camberwell, Victoria 3124,
Australia (a division of Pearson Australia Group Pty. Ltd.)
Penguin Books India Pvt. Ltd., 11 Community Centre, Panchsheel Park,
New Delhi – 110 017, India
Penguin Group (NZ), 67 Apollo Drive, Rosedale, North Shore 0632, New Zealand
(a division of Pearson New Zealand Ltd.)
Penguin Books (South Africa) (Pty.) Ltd., 24 Sturdee Avenue, Rosebank,
Johannesburg 2196, South Africa

Penguin Books Ltd., Registered Offices: 80 Strand, London WC2R 0RL, England

Published by Plume, a member of Penguin Group (USA) Inc. Originally published
in Great Britain as *The Spiritual Teachings of the Tao* by Hodder and Stoughton.

First American Printing, April 2003
15 14 13 12 11 10 9 8 7

A CIP catalogue record for this title is available from the British Library

ISBN 0-340-73319-5 (hc.)
ISBN 978-0-452-28403-6 (pbk.)

Printed in the United States of America

Contents

Acknowledgements

The author would like to thank the following people for helping in the creation of this book and audiotape:

Rowena Webb, my editor at Hodder and Stoughton, who had the courage to commission this series.

Rupert Lancaster, Editor of Hodder Audio, for his support and help on the audio version.

My friends who read early drafts and gave valuable suggestions.

My agent Liv Blumer for all her help and support.

Mick Tomlinson of Rising Dragon Tai Chi for showing me how to use Tai Chi principles in life.

Alex de Kang Zheng for the Chinese calligraphy.

Faber and Faber for permission to quote from 'In Memory of W. B. Yeats' from *Collected Poems* by W. H. Auden.

J. M. Dent, publishers, for allowing me to quote from Dylan Thomas's poem, 'The Force That through the Green Fuse'.

And finally my wife Jo who helped edit the Chuang Tzu texts and put up with all my nonsense.

In the deserts of the heart
Let the healing fountain start,
In the prison of his days
Teach the free man how to praise.
                    W.H AUDEN

The sound of rain needs no translation.
                    ROSHI MORIMOTO

Preface

- ◆ uniting mind, body and spirit
- ◆ the integration of self
- ◆ enjoying a long and healthy life
- ◆ having an awareness of our place in the universe
- ◆ appreciating the beauty and wonder of nature

Attaining these states of being, and with them to experience the sheer pleasure of existence, must be one of our greatest aims. No matter how difficult or even impossible it appears to attain such bliss, we have never stopped wanting to find a way to live a completely harmonious life.

Over 2,500 years ago Chinese thinkers found and explored a way of experiencing life that delivered just these benefits. They believed there was a Tao (pronounced 'dow'), or Way of Nature, that permeated all of existence, and that it was possible for anyone to follow or imitate this Tao in order to find a profound balance and serenity in life.

The Tao of Nature they followed has unique and mysterious powers of transformation and change, so that anyone who finds life unsatisfactory can, by following this Tao, discover a practice of self-cultivation that reverses bad habits and establishes a new and better way of living.

I'm not writing this book as an objective scholar of Chinese philosophy, but as someone who has tried, over the past few years, to put these Taoist ways into practice in daily life. I'm a Tai Chi 'player', I meditate when I can find the time, and I try to live by the Taoist teachings. My aim in this book is to explain Taoism and to show how useful and effective it can be.

Taoism says that happiness is to be found in the here and now, in our mundane physical world, and not in an afterlife, or in a spiritual union with God. Because of this, it accepts the physical side of life, and has never lost a healthy and ecological view of nature. I believe that Taoism is a philosophy whose time has come, and it contains within its teachings the seeds for a regeneration of the Western mind and soul.

Part One of this book, 'The Art Of Living', introduces the subject, examines the concept of the Tao, and explains the relevance the Tao of Nature had for the ancient people who found it and lived it.

Part One also examines the relevance of the Tao for contemporary living, and explains why its teaching is a living philosophy that has not dated. It is used daily in the practices of Feng Shui, Tai Chi Chuan, acupuncture and traditional chinese medicine, which have gained wide acceptance and popularity in the West over the past fifty years.

Part Two, *The Book Of Chuang Tzu*, is a new version of the writings of the liveliest and wittiest of the Taoist philosophers, Chuang Tzu (whose name means Master Chuang), who lived in the fourth century BCE (before the Christian era). Chuang Tzu's book, the oldest classic of philosophical Taoism, is a collection of parables, fables, anecdotes, jokes and dialogues that illuminates the Tao in an original and inventive style.

The Book of Chuang Tzu is best read in small chunks, perhaps before going to bed, or on the bus or train. It can be used as a spiritual tonic or as a guide to life. Ideally it shouldn't be read like a novel or a continuous work. Although I've edited the text into sixteen thematic chapters and put them in a new order, there's no need to read the work in the order I've given. You can dive in anywhere and appreciate Chuang Tzu's humour and poetry.

PART ONE

The Art of Living

I

A Minor Dilemma

The *Tao Te Ching* (pronounced 'dow day jing'), the ancient 'bible' of philosophical Taoism, says,

> *The Tao that can be talked about is not the real Tao.*

and

> *He who knows does not speak,*
> *he who speaks does not know.*

This makes it rather difficult for anyone to write a book about the Tao. If you presume to write about it, then, according to the *Tao Te Ching*, you can't be writing about the real Tao, and the very fact of your attempting to write about it already makes you suspect.

How can I get out of this dilemma, because I do want to write about the Tao and hope that what I write will be of some use in understanding this ancient and vibrant way of thinking and living? Perhaps Chuang Tzu, whose book I have edited and rewritten as Part Two of this work, can give me some advice. After all, Chuang Tzu and his followers wrote about the Tao to communicate their ideas and methods:

> *The world thinks the most valuable exhibition of Tao is found*
> *in its classic books. But books are only a collection of words.*
> *Words are valuable: what is valuable in them is the ideas they*

convey. But those ideas are a sequence of something else, and that something else can't be conveyed by words.

When the world, because of the value it attaches to words, commits those words to books, the thing it so values them for may not deserve to be valued. Because what the world values isn't what is really valuable.

And Chuang Tzu also writes:

Fishing baskets are for catching fish. But when the fish are caught, you forget the baskets. Snares are for catching hares, but when the hares are trapped, you forget the snares. Words are for conveying ideas, but when the ideas are understood, you forget the words. How I'd love to talk with someone who's forgotten all the words!

I'd like to use some good and simple words of my own to convey some of these valuable ideas, and through these ideas I hope we can at least get a fleeting glimpse of the mysterious 'something else' that Chuang Tzu refers to. The ultimate stage is when we too can learn to forget the words, and penetrate directly to the reality of Tao.

2

My Story

I've been reading Chuang Tzu since 1972, and have always been amused and charmed by his fantastic characters, situations and dialogues. Every time I open his book it brings a smile of recognition to my face. So when the success of *The Spiritual Teachings of Marcus Aurelius* gave me the chance to do a book on Taoism, I chose this work, partly because of my affection for it, but mainly because of the instruction it has given me for nearly thirty years. My debt to Chinese sages like Confucius, Mencius, Lao Tzu, Chuang Tzu, and the English translators who have made their work available is immense.

From these sages, both Confucian and Taoist, I've learned innumerable lessons of life, from how to look frankly at death to how to deal with family problems. They showed me a different way to think about money and fame, and how to look after my body and mind. I've tried, in the last few years, to put this teaching into practice in all parts of my life.

My practice includes Tai Chi and Chi Kung, forms of energy exercise, as well as meditation and breathing exercises. I'm also lucky in that my wife is a yoga teacher, and I've been able to attend her classes. The cumulative result of these activities, accompanied by a sensible life-style, is quite striking. I've lost weight without dieting, my muscles, particularly my leg muscles, have become stronger, and my body has gained in overall flexibility. Joints that were stiff have given way, and ones that remain stiff have softened.

I believe these practices, allied to a new way of looking at the world, have changed my entire approach to life, and the last few years have been among the happiest of my life. Whether this is entirely due to Taoism I can't say, but I do know that my body, mind and spirit have found a serenity and harmony that were missing in earlier years.

What makes Taoist practices so accessible and practical is that they can sit quite easily alongside other beliefs and activities without coming into conflict. I'm a non-practising Jew, but there's nothing in Taoism that would conflict with Jewish values and practices if I decide to join a synagogue. If anything, the ethical values of Taoism are on a par with Judeo-Christian ethics.

The reverence and devotion that the Taoists express for the Tao has shown me that the kinds of feelings my ancestors had for God, for a power greater than their small selves, are feelings that are still available to me, even if I express them to the power of the universe and not to a personal God.

Access to these feelings has helped to free my soul, and I feel a debt of gratitude to the Taoists, whose writings have shown me how to gain access to these emotions. Taoists were often great poets, and Chuang Tzu was no exception. He has been called the finest of all Chinese poets, and could express with great facility deep feelings about life. His understanding is always profound and insightful:

The Master said, 'In the world there are two great principles: one is the requirement implanted in our nature and the other is the conviction of what's right.

'The love of a daughter for her parents is implanted in her, and can never be erased from her heart. That a minister should serve his ruler is what's right, and he can't escape this obligation. These are called the great universal principles.

'Therefore a daughter finds peace in serving her parents wherever they may be, and this is the height of devotion. Similarly, a minister finds peace in serving his ruler, whatever the matter, and this is the height of loyalty.

'When you simply obey the commands of your heart, thoughts of sorrow and joy don't arise. There's no alternative to acting as you do, and you accept this as your destiny. This is the perfection of virtue.

'As a minister and a son you must do what can't be avoided. Absorb yourself in your mission and ignore your own self. When will you have time to think of loving life or hating death?

'Act like this and all will be well.'

What I admire about the Taoists is that they found a simple and satisfying solution to life, without ignoring its great complexity. There is a story that encapsulates this,

A wealthy merchant visited a sage and asked him to make a wall-hanging, a beautiful work of calligraphy for his family.

'I want you to write the recipe for happiness,' said the merchant.

The sage told him it would be ready in a week. When the merchant returned, the sage showed him the work. It said,

> Father dies.
> Son dies.

The merchant was furious. 'What kind of recipe is this for happiness!'

The sage picked up his brush, dipped it in ink, and wrote,

> *Son dies.*
> *Father dies.*

'Would you prefer it in this order?'

The Taoist recipe for happiness is to follow the Natural Way, not to place yourself in opposition to the way things flow, but to plant yourself right in the midst of that flow, and not only to accept it but to revel in it. Whether people today are able to get back to that simplicity is questionable, since we have grown very cynical and admire the complex and difficult, even when these rarely give us anything positive in return.

I hope this book can show people a way to approach Taoist simplicity without necessarily giving up their own ideas about religion, science or philosophy. But it will very likely make them question some of their beliefs, and perhaps work for change. The book will try to answer, with more clarity than Chuang Tzu might approve of, the most obvious questions that anyone could ask:

- ◆ What is the Tao?
- ◆ Where does it come from?
- ◆ What does it do?
- ◆ Why be interested in it?

To be clear about something like the Tao, whose beginning and essence lie in obscurity and darkness, may be an impossible (and perhaps unnecessary) task, but even if we only illuminate that darkness sufficiently to know where we must explore in future, then we will have done enough to justify the attempt.

3

In Search of the Tao

Why do Taoists say that we can't talk about the real Tao? It's because the real Tao isn't a concept, and therefore words can't describe it. It's something that existed before there were words, before there was human speech, before there was even thought. It's something that must be lived and experienced and not just talked about.

The word Tao in Chinese originally meant road, path, track or course. Later it came to mean way, in the sense of a way of looking at the world, a certain attitude of mind, a philosophy. This is how it is written in Chinese:

Tao

Chuang Tzu discovered his Tao during the fourth century BCE, an era in China known as the 'Warring States' period, a time of political, social and moral chaos. In this confused and dangerous time, many competing schools of philosophy grew up, and each of these 'Hundred Schools' had its own particular 'Way' which it thought society should follow.

Scholars would travel from state to state trying to convince the local rulers to put their philosophy into practice as a means of ordering the state and political life.

All Chinese philosophy has tried to unify Heaven, Earth and mankind, the sublime and the mundane, the material and the spiritual. The Chinese have always tried to integrate man and nature, knowing that man and nature are not two things, two separate entities, but are always one. The ancient Chinese had a holistic, ecological view of life, in which our existence on earth only makes sense if it is linked with the sun, the moon and the stars, the wind and the rain, and all the other processes of nature. Alone, we are nothing. They knew that all life depended on all other life for its existence, and that thinking of things as separate is only possible intellectually. In reality nothing can be separated.

4

Confucius

The earliest philosopher in China, and the most famous, is Confucius. Confucius lived from 551 to 479 BCE, so he pre-dated Chuang Tzu by well over 100 years, but his students and his philosophy were still very much alive during Chuang Tzu's time.

Confucius had a noble lineage, but grew up in a poor family. He became a scholar, and took it on himself single-handedly to reform the sixth century Chinese world. That world was one of increasing chaos and warfare as the Chou king lost his power over the large and small fiefdoms that comprised his kingdom. As they jockeyed for power, all the old religious traditions and values were abandoned, and replaced by naked aggression and power. Old ideas of human nature were thrown aside and philosophy was born from the need to discover the true nature of a human being.

Confucius believed that the past held the key to this knowledge, and he went back to the ancient rituals and writings to discover what had been lost. He eventually edited (and probably rewrote) these classics and held them, and their authors, the ancient sage-kings and emperors, as examples of statesmanship to the contemporary princes and war-lords.

He was desperate to gain a position of power and influence so that he could put his ideas into practice, but no prince would give him anything but nominal power, and he spent many frustrating years travelling from state to state trying to convince the rulers to follow his Way, the Way of Heaven. A number of the Chuang Tzu stories about Confucius detail his adventures and difficulties during this time.

Confucius gathered many disciples and students, and he was the first teacher to start a school to train young men for government positions, so they could take his principles and put them into practice, revolutionising the states from within. In this he was very successful, and Confucianism became the official state religion some 300 years after his death. China, and all the South-east Asian countries influenced by Chinese culture, including Japan, Vietnam, Korea, Laos and Thailand, have all been strongly influenced by this teacher's ideas and values. A number of Confucius' students feature in Chuang Tzu's stories.

Confucius' Way of Heaven was based on the idea of a noble man, the superior man. Previously a noble man was a nobleman, made that way by birth and family, and not by merit or intellectual ability. But Confucius said that a noble man could come from any stratum of society, and what mattered was how he treated other people. If he was a moral person, and acted unselfishly, kindly, loyally and with justice, then he was a true noble man.

Confucius set up strict conventional rules of morality that the superior man had to follow, and it is these rules of goodness and justice that Chuang Tzu makes so much fun of in his writings. To Chuang Tzu these conventions of morality were too artificial, and could easily be imitated from the outside and not felt from the inside. Consequently it was easy for people to be hypocritical in their dealings with others but still consider themselves superior.

To make things slightly more complicated, in some of the Chuang Tzu stories Confucius is either searching himself for the Tao, or has become a convert to Taoism and is giving his students Taoist teaching. These stories show Chuang Tzu clearly making fun of Confucius, but in many of the stories there is a deep admiration for the man who was a pioneer and lived through difficult times without ever relinquishing his principles. The fact is that Confucius did teach his students to work and struggle hard, and it was due to their efforts that Confucianism overtook Taoism to become the first official state philosophy/religion after 140 BCE.

5

Chuang Tzu

Chuang Tzu, whose dates may perhaps be 369–286 BCE, became known to later Taoists as the True Man of Tao. He was one of the earliest philosophers of the Way and is considered one of the three founders of Philosophical Taoism (the others being Lao Tzu and Lieh Tzu).

All we know of his life is that he was born in a town called Meng, got married, had children and held a minor government job. Refusing wealth, power and title he once declined a powerful position from the King of Chu, a story told in Chapter 2, Perfect Happiness.

His book, *The Book Of Chuang Tzu*, says of him:

Chuang Tzu discussed the Tao using strange and mysterious expressions, wild and extravagant words. He saw the whole world as sunk in stupidity and incapable of understanding anything sensible. So he enjoyed himself with the spirits of Heaven and Earth, but didn't consider himself superior to ordinary life.

Though his writings may appear sparkling trifles, his use of words, and his surprising turns and changes, are ever-varying. The fullness and completeness of his ideas can't be exhausted.

Above, he seeks delight in Great Tao; below, he looks kindly on those who consider life and death as having neither beginning nor end. Contemplating the origin of all things, he's comprehensive and great, opening up new views: deep, vast and free.

We can say that he was in harmony with Great Tao itself, carrying our thoughts to range and play in the sublime. Nevertheless, on the subject of transformation, and freedom from the enslavement to things, his principles are inexhaustible, and are wholly his own. His ideas are subtle and profound, and can never be fully explained.

Chuang Tzu wasn't interested in influencing rulers to take up the Tao, nor is his book addressed to sages, real or potential, like the *Tao Te Ching*. Instead, and remarkably for the period he wrote in, when the nobility was effectively the only class holding power, his book seems to be addressed to ordinary individuals.

He's aware that he himself holds knowledge and understanding that's rare in the world, and if people can be persuaded to use that knowledge and discover it in themselves, then they can find a way, in fact the Way, to bring satisfaction and contentment to their lives, instead of the anguish and difficulties that many people seem to endure.

Chuang Tzu didn't encourage his contemporaries to take up official positions, since he believed this would just give them trouble and shorten their lives. He gave the same advice on wealth and fame. He didn't want people to pursue false gods, the way we do, but to find a kind of god in themselves, Tao, and to gain a real sense of pleasure and happiness in life.

Like us, he doesn't have faith in politics and leaders. I get the sense that, to Chuang Tzu, society, as a collective, is probably beyond help. But society is made up of individuals, and if each individual can find Tao, then eventually society can become completely transformed.

Chuang Tzu was that rarity, a poet-philosopher, and his dates are not that much later than our other well-known philosopher-poet, Plato. Chuang Tzu's interest was in illuminating the Tao, spreading the word about this mysterious yet worldly philosophy and way of living. But he wanted to do this through poetry and humour, and not as a work of scripture. The *Tao Te Ching* impressively fulfils that role.

Chuang Tzu writes about a quirky mob of mystics, teachers, cripples, hermits, princes, fish, birds, philosophers, sages, farmers, shepherds, wheelwrights, carpenters and cooks, in short, funny and trenchant stories and dialogues that make the Tao come alive. In writing like this, he was unique among philosophers, and it's a tribute to his ability that these texts are so striking and vital 2,300 years after they were written. The parallels between his thought and ours, given the gap of time, language and culture, I find extraordinary.

6

Twenty-first Century Chuang Tzu

Part Two of this book is my version of Chuang Tzu's work. I've selected about half of his writings and placed them in sixteen thematic chapters. A Note on the Text at the end of Part One goes into more detail.

Since I don't read Chinese my aim in making this new version is clearly not to be philologically correct. Instead, I've tried to look at the texts from the inside, both the inside of Chuang Tzu's mind (as much as that's possible) to understand what he is getting at, and from inside my own body and mind, since as a Tai Chi 'player' and meditator I bring my own practice and insights to the work. To me, *The Book of Chuang Tzu* is not an academic work of ancient philosophy, but a handbook and guide to contemporary living.

7

The Body of the Tao

The Taoists never fell into the intellectual trap of consider-ing the opposition of body and mind, or material and spiritual, or Heaven and Earth, as being true opposites, as Western and Christian thought dangerously did. These dual-istic splits have damaged us because for hundreds of years we have viewed the body as the home of corruption and evil, and the spirit as the home of the higher qualities and the divine. We often act as if body and soul are two rivals fight-ing for ultimate control, instead of comprehending their underlying unity. The Taoists realised that all opposites aren't opponents that must clash but are part of a dynamic balance of existence, necessary to create and sustain life.

Rather than judging that the mind or spirit was higher and better than the body or matter, and therefore elevating the spiritual as an ideal to aspire to and denigrating the body as a corrupting influence to avoid, the Chinese accepted that mind and body, spiritual and material, were both acceptable, both necessary, both equal. All opposites are in reality one thing, not two, and they looked for the source of that unity.

This search, which probably began around the sixth cen-tury BCE, was paralleled at virtually the same time in the Greek-speaking Middle East, where the first Hellenic philoso-phers, the so-called Pre-Socratics, were engaged on the same quest. This period, the sixth to fifth centuries BCE, was a time of world-wide intellectual and spiritual ferment that brought forth the Buddha in India, the second Prophet Isaiah in Israel, Pythagoras in Greece, Zoroaster in Persia, and the Chinese philosophers Confucius and Lao Tzu.

The early Greek philosophers wanted to look beyond the dazzling and numberless appearances of life to discover what it was they all held in common. What was the substance, the reality, behind the façade of appearances? Different philosophers came up with different ideas, which ranged from water, earth, air, and fire, (later joined together as the four elements) to more subtle ideas like the mind, or the early conception of atoms.

Chinese thinkers were also searching for this universal substance and reality, and they found it in something they called chi, which translates as breath, or energy. This is its Chinese character:

Chi

Chi is the energy permeating and organising all of existence, including our own bodies. It's responsible for circulation, not only the circulation of breath, blood and the other fluids in our body, but the circulation of the wind and rain, the sun and the moon. It's from this conception of chi that the Chinese developed their system of medicine.

Chi is everywhere and in everything, but it didn't come into existence by itself. It needed a source, the source of reality, and the Chinese called this source Tao. Unlike chi, which is physical and can be felt and measured, Tao is neither physical nor spiritual. Instead, paradoxically, it's both physical and spiritual yet neither physical nor spiritual.

This sounds like gobbledegook, and that's why the ancients said that it isn't possible to talk about Tao. Because it's impossible to conceive of anything that is neither physical nor spiritual, we are left trying hopelessly through the means of paradox and negative description to explain what Tao isn't. How can one define the indefinable?

The reason we can't describe Tao is because it is purely potential – it's the potential and orderly power that produces all things physical and spiritual. The Taoists believe that Tao is the origin and source of the entire universe, and everything in it. We can think of it as primeval chaos, but this chaos isn't totally anarchic, since it has within it the principle of order. And out of this primeval chaos evolves the spontaneous creation that has unfolded all life, including life on Earth, and especially for us consciousness, our own creative source.

But Tao doesn't actually do anything or produce anything – it isn't active, nor does it rest. It merely creates the conditions in which activity can take place, an activity that is continuously flowing and changing. Tao is formless and has no shape. Being formless it can't be seen, heard or touched. It has no existence or being, but is primal Non-existence. Taoists believe that from this Non-existence and Non-being it creates all existence and all being. It endlessly and changelessly inhabits the void, or emptiness, and it's from this non-location that it performs its daily miracles.

The ancient Chinese philosophers who discovered this creative source of the universe must have found it through observing life around them, in water and light, in plants and animals, in contemplation of the stars and Heavenly bodies, but also by filtering what they observed and discovered through a trance-like meditation on their own existence: their senses, minds and bodies. The Taoist highly values this subjective knowledge, as the Tao Te Ching declares:

How do I know the Tao of all things at the beginning?
By what is within.

The Taoist knows that Tao operates everywhere, so that its influence is in the Heavens and his own body at the same time. He discovers Tao's laws and secrets within himself partly by empirical observation of nature, including human nature, and partly by deep meditation, which in silence and stillness leads to a mystical vision of unity.

The early Taoists first tried to understand in themselves how this principle worked, to enable them to explain it to others, and to put it to use in all aspects of their lives.

When this principle became elaborated in what we now call Taoism, the philosophy became a Way of Nature, a way of aligning with the natural flow of the universe, the cyclical way things grow and develop. Taoists follow the workings of the Tao in nature, and don't presume to control it as we do in the West. Their aim is to let human nature become free so that its living potential can flower and become fully realised. They believe that nature has to be accepted, trusted and worked with rather than fought against. Taoism is not only a way of looking at the world and understanding it, but more importantly, an effective and real way of acting and living.

Because Taoism is a true marriage of mind, body and spirit, it has never excluded the body as a source of importance, interest, wonder and pleasure. In many ways the body in Taoism is given precedence over the mind, and this respect for the body enabled the early Taoists to discover secrets of diet, breathing, meditation, exercise, medicine and sexuality.

This ancient knowledge is proving its value today in the forms of acupuncture, massage, herbal medicine, Tai Chi Chuan, Chi Kung and Feng Shui, all of which have become increasingly popular. The West has discovered how effective and powerful these practices are, and their popularity is due to the positive effect these disciplines have on our well-being.

The importance of the body in Taoism gives it a concrete down-to-earth quality that is missing in many other philosophies. Unlike philosophies and religions that believe the world is either an illusion or the source of corruption, Taoism accepts that our mundane worldly life is not only real but must be a source of happiness if life is to be worth living.

Consequently there is a very basic and fundamental side to Taoism that goes to the very root of human existence. This makes its ideas and practices easily understood and extremely accessible. Because Taoism was never afflicted with the mind–body split of the West, it has retained a healthy and holistic attitude to nature and the universe, an attitude that contains the possibility of healing the Western soul.

I believe that in the twenty-first century we will be increasingly in need of a way to unify our lives and to maintain a real and durable connection with nature, in the face of a proliferating technology that continues to dominate our lives. Unless we are able to see and feel the primal living connection between ourselves and the rest of creation, we will find ourselves increasingly cut off from organic existence, and will face the threat of turning into mindlessly driven machine operators in an increasingly oppressive machine-dominated world, which will continue in the mistaken attempt to completely control the natural world.

Having created thinking machines in our own image, we should be aware that their future development must be towards replacing us, something that has already happened to the logical and calculating functions of the brain. Computers largely do this work for us, and, unless we can develop our inherent qualities of intuitive wisdom and creativity to evolve to a different level, they will very likely make us redundant.

By seeking the Tao of nature in ourselves, we can develop more understanding about how to tap into our intuitive selves, and by extending our selves beyond our small egos, can integrate better with other creatures and things. Through this we can discover personal meaning and purpose in a world increasingly devoid of meaning.

This is one of the ways in which Chuang Tzu described his Way, or Tao:

This is the Great Tao.
It has both reality and substance, but it does nothing
and has no material form.
A teacher can transmit it,
but can't guarantee its reception.
It can be found, but it can't be seen:
it is its own source, its own root.
Before there was Heaven and Earth,
from of old, there it was,
eternally existing.

From it came the mysterious existence of spirit,
from it came the mysterious existence of God.
It produced Heaven and Earth.
It is far above, yet can't be considered high.
It is below all space, yet can't be considered deep.
It was born before Heaven and Earth,
yet you can't say it's existed for long.
It's older than the oldest antiquity,
yet you can't call it old.

No one knows its beginning,
no one knows its end.
You listen for it,
but can't hear its sound.
You look for it,
but can't perceive its shape.

It fills Heaven and Earth and envelops everything within the universe.

To approach something as mysterious, obscure and fugitive as Tao directly is of no use, since it will disperse and disappear in front of us. Instead we need to make a more subtle and indirect approach, spiralling towards it in the same way that it spirals all life into existence.

8

Why a Tree Is Not a Tree

It is mid-morning on a beautiful and placid summer's day. The warm sun flits between clouds dotted against a light blue sky. When the sun breaks free of the clouds, a shimmering light strikes the trees, turning the leaves at the top a bright green, leaving those on the bottom branches a darker, heavier colour, shading into the brown of the trunk. It's a feast for the eyes.

The Tao is in these trees, just as it's in all of nature. It's also in human nature, in me, the observer (who is also present, simultaneously subject and object) in this urban park. A tree exists, I exist, and the Tao exists in us both, but when I want to talk or write about any one of these three, I must use symbols – words – and those words take me away from the reality of the Tao, the tree and me.

I'd like to explore how this happens. In front of me is a large tree. It's perfectly real, and if I approach closely I can feel the rough bark of its trunk and the silken surface of its leaves. But the word that we use – 'tree' – has no bark or leaves. It's two sounds, something like 'tuh ree', that by convention we've agreed will stand for, or symbolise, the concept of a tree. But if I repeat these two sounds over and over again – tuh ree tuh ree tuh ree tuh ree tuh ree tuh ree tuh ree tuh ree – they soon become just meaningless noise and lose all connection with that magnificent creation standing in front of me.

We decide, by convention, to assign meaning to things. These two sounds, tuh ree, we've agreed will stand as a symbol for a large wooded plant rooted in the earth. All languages are sets of symbols to describe the universe, and, as Chuang Tzu says, the universe both emanates from, and is, the Tao. To use human language to encompass and describe this non-material origin of everything is logically suspect. Our language really breaks down in trying to describe it, but because language comprises symbols that the mind can handle, we delude ourselves into thinking that our words are real in the same way that the tree is real.

By calling a tree a tree, by giving it a name so we can talk about it, we consider it in isolation in our minds. We make it a thing, and separate it from the earth that it stands in and the sky that nourishes it. We abstract it from the environment that in reality it can't be separated from. Only our minds can make this artificial separation, and be fooled by it. The tree isn't an object, a thing, but is a process of transformation, a constant flowing and a becoming.

Every year, I see this tree going through its annual cyclic process of budding in spring, flowering in summer, decaying and shedding its leaves in autumn, and resting in a barren state throughout the winter, until the green regeneration miraculously returns again in spring. Over the longer cycle of time, I know that even before I was born, this tree started its life as a tiny seed, which has grown and developed into a mature tree, and, barring a hurricane or other disaster, at some time in the future it will eventually decline and die. As a creature existing in time, the tree is much more of an event than an object.

And I, the person looking at it, am also subject to these cycles – of birth, growth, development and eventual decline and death. I too am in process, am flowing, constantly altering, from the cells that renew themselves on a daily basis to hair that continues to grey with every passing year. And, like the tree, I too am an event and not an object or a thing that can be considered in separation from my environment. Because if I want to take a walk, I need the earth to support me, and when I breathe I need the air to sustain me. Our minds fool us into thinking that we are independent, separate creatures, an island of ego inside our skin, when in reality we are all part of a vast web of relationships, and if these relationships become degraded and destroyed, we too will be destroyed.

Therefore, the tree that can be talked about is not the real tree. Reality can't be enclosed and described by words. Symbols aren't real in the way that a tree is real, and however much we may delude ourselves that they are, we'll eventually find that the word 'water' won't quench our thirst, and eating dollar bills won't satisfy our hunger.

So 'the Tao' that we can talk about is not real Tao, because any Tao that we can conceive of is merely a concept of 'the Tao' in our minds and not Tao itself. What Tao is we must discover in some other way, without relying on language and symbol. We need to experience life directly, and it's in that experience that we approach closer to it.

9

Taste and See

I'd like, with your help, to conduct a demonstration in existence, or the state of 'isness'. To take part, you must put your book down and go and pour yourself a glass of drinking water. When you've done this, pick up the glass, bring it to your mouth, let the water flow through your lips, and drink.

Even if I were Shakespeare himself I couldn't describe the temperature or taste of that water when it splashes on your tongue. Only you can say whether the water is warm or cool, fresh or stale, still or bubbly. Only you have this knowledge, which can't be shared with anyone else. Words can only describe ideas and concepts, they're unable to express the sensation of raw experience, of the smoothness of the glass on your lips, its weight when raised by your hand or the feeling of the liquid flowing into your mouth and down your throat. So, how did it taste? You'll find you can't describe it, and there's no way that anyone else can find out. The only thing I can do is drink my own and find out for myself what it tastes like. In this, as in so many other things in life, we're on our own. Only you can taste the living water – no one can taste it for you. Life is here to be experienced, but when we stand aside from it and just think about it, try to understand it only with words, then we isolate ourselves from nature, both the widest nature and our own human nature, and we create feelings of isolation, fear, alienation, insecurity and separation.

Only you can have this knowledge, which can't be shared with another. This is subjective knowledge, the knowledge of reality, of the real, and not only is it our only true knowledge, it's also the knowledge of Tao.

IO

Subjective and Objective Knowledge

There's a limit to life, but to knowledge there's no limit. Using what's limited to seek out the unlimited is futile. And if, knowing this, we still act according to knowledge, then danger can't be avoided.

When she was seven, I asked my youngest daughter the first question of the ancient Greek philosophers, 'What's the world made of?' and she gave me the answer, 'The world is made of feelings – happy and sad, fear and anger.' Her answer surprised me, not only because it wasn't what I was expecting, but also because it was so true.

Descartes famously said, 'I think, therefore I am', but my daughter says, 'I feel, therefore I am.' Now, both of these statements are partly right, because thinking and feeling share the conscious function of our minds, but my daughter's insight is more wholesome than Descartes', because his premise forced a deep cleavage in our association between body and mind, whereas my daughter intuitively keeps body and mind together, since both mind and body experience feelings directly. If we want to reduce both of these statements to an even more basic level we could say, 'I breathe, therefore I am.' Thinking, feeling and breathing can in turn all be reduced to a common source, the energy operating in the universe:

I am energy
I am Tao
I am
I

My daughter's answer reveals one side of real knowledge, the subjective knowledge of existence. Knowledge is conventionally considered to be of two kinds: subjective and objective, knowing what and knowing how, having and being. The 'what' type is objective knowledge that you can acquire and have. It's the analytical knowledge of science, of facts that can be measured, calculated and tested, and so is almost the only knowledge taught in schools.

This knowledge traditionally uses a reductionist method to break reality into separate parts, and then looks at each of these in isolation from the remainder. It's a process that goes deeper and deeper into the smallest parts, increasingly isolating those parts from the whole. It provides detailed knowledge of the isolated part, but finds it more difficult to relate that part to others. This knowledge is powerful and effective, for it's given us Western medicine, technology, and extensive control over the natural world.

The other kind of knowledge is 'how', knowledge as experience, knowledge of being, of body, mind and soul that you can only discover for and in yourself. Schools rarely attempt to deal with this kind of knowledge, and they often inhibit children from learning methods to discover this kind of real knowledge. True knowledge is empowering for the individual and represents real personal power.

Here's an example of the subjective, 'how' kind of knowledge from Chuang Tzu. A wheelwright is explaining his craft:

'In making a wheel, if I go at it gently, it's certainly pleasant enough, but the workmanship isn't very strong. If I have to

push forcefully, that's an effort and the joints won't fit well. Neither too gentle nor too forceful: my hand knows how to do it in harmony with my heart, and a fine wheel is produced.

'But I can't tell you how to do it in words – there's a certain knack to it. I can't even teach this knack to my son, nor can my son learn it from me. That's why I'm seventy years old and am still making wheels.'

It is this 'knack' of living, a true art of living, that the Taoists were interested in discovering and using. This required making a deep inner journey to find the intuitive and unconscious knowledge of how their bodies and minds operated. In making this journey they discovered that their bodies and minds corresponded in a miraculous and organic way with the rest of creation. They saw that all life, not just human life, was in a profound union with the entire universe. They saw no difference between how their organism maintained itself in life and the way the universe itself maintained all of existence. This revelation was holistic, subtle, profound, mysterious, and was a mixture of both subjective and objective knowledge, which in the Tao became harmonised as one.

Our culture isn't comfortable with deep subjective experience, in which artistic, religious and mystical feelings are found. We're often wary of exploring this interior life, because we're afraid of what may be lurking there: fears and insecurities, repressed feelings of sexuality or anger. This is because the subjective life is home to the unconscious, that powerful, dark and hidden side of our mind, which is also the source of our creativity.

Often scientists and others who are more comfortable with objective knowledge forget that creativity not only generates artistic and mystical feelings but also includes their own scientific creativity, as the career of Albert Einstein makes very clear. Einstein's important discoveries were all made first in his mind, through subjective unconscious reflection. Only later did he go to the trouble of testing them 'objectively'.

We have lived in a materialistic, scientific culture for so long that objective knowledge is king, and the subjective is denigrated and considered suspect and unreliable. I looked up 'objective' in my dictionary of philosophy and the definition read, 'Having a real existence as opposed to a merely subjective one.'

Our culture considers the subjective as unreal and only the objective as real. But how does anyone, whether scientist or mystic, make sense of the world except through subjective vision? We know that true objectivity is impossible, that the presence of the observer always changes what is observed, so subjective vision is really all we have to make sense of the world. Yet our education succeeds in making us wary and mistrustful of our own subjective feelings and insights. This mistrust of our deepest selves, and the doubts raised by it, are the source of many of our spiritual problems.

We need to find a better balance between these two kinds of knowledge, so that truths from both can co-exist, and we can find trust not only in the objective truths of science, but also in our own subjective feelings and insights. To the Taoist these subjective truths must be given a higher priority. Chuang Tzu put it like this,

The person who uses only the vision of his eyes is conditioned purely by what he sees. But it's the intuition of the spirit that perceives reality.

The wise have known for a long time that what we know through our eyes isn't equal to the intuition of our spirit. Yet most people rely only on what they see, and lose themselves in external things. Isn't this sad?

II

Spontaneity

My daughter once said to me, 'When I was born, you and Mummy came alive.' Remarkably, she was echoing a saying of Chuang Tzu:

Heaven, earth and I were produced together,
and all life and I are one.

They both express that wholly subjective feeling of unity, of being at one with the universe, something we all feel when we're very young, but which we soon forget. Freud said that an unborn child and young infant experience an 'oceanic consciousness' where all feelings are diffuse and undifferentiated, and there are no boundaries between the infant and the rest of the world. All experiences, whether happening inside or outside the body, are identified by the baby as coming from one source.

What my daughter and Chuang Tzu experienced is the feeling that our birth brings the entire universe into existence with us. It's possible that when my daughter grows up, she may well forget this feeling, and will instead feel cut off, alienated, separate from other people and from the universe, will feel, like many of us, 'a stranger in a strange land.' My hope is that one day she will read this book, and, remembering how she once had this cosmic sensation, may wonder whether it's possible to recapture that wonderful feeling.

This is where the Taoists can be helpful. They worked out a means of transformation through self-cultivation, a possibility of reversing, of getting back to that original state of unity of childhood, without reverting to a false and naïve innocence. Oddly enough, they share a view of children with the radical Jewish teacher Jesus of Galilee:

Truly, I say to you, unless you turn and become like children, you will never enter the Kingdom of Heaven.

Like Jesus, the Taoists believe that as children we retain a purer sense of the primal power of life, but that, as we grow up, society, with its strong conditioning of mind and body, creates a false view of life, an illusion-led existence which takes us further and further away from the original essence we were born with. As Chuang Tzu says,

Can you become like a little child?

A child can scream its head off all day without becoming hoarse – so perfect is its harmony. It can clench its fists all day without relaxing its grip – so intense is its vital power. It can stare all day without moving its eyes – so unconcerned is it by the outside world. It walks but doesn't know where. It rests where it's placed, but doesn't know why. It unconsciously mingles with things, and just follows their flow.

Jung said that we have four different mental functions: thinking, feeling, sense and intuition. When we're born, our thinking function is the least developed, because our brain, in particular the forebrain, is still in growth and development, and continues to develop for a further forty years.

Infants operate on the three remaining functions of feeling, sense, and intuition, and utilise only the primitive brain, the brain stem, for their 'thinking'. The brain stem operates the autonomous functions of the body such as the blood flow, body temperature, hormone releasing, digestion, breathing and so on. With the unconscious mind maintaining its body, the child is free to explore its world unthinkingly.

The Taoist desire to transform or revert to a state of infancy means giving up an unnecessary and unhealthy reliance on the thinking function, and utilising much more the intuitive and unconscious aspects of our being. Thinking does have an important role to play, but only when we need to use it specifically. When I have to write an introduction like this, I rely very heavily on this thinking function. I note down possible themes or chapter headings, then consider what order I need to place them in. I have deliberately to recall ideas I want to write about, and remind myself if I've forgotten any, or duplicated others. This linear shuffling process is rational thinking, and involves the logical, conscious part of the brain. We particularly use this brain function when calculating numbers and measuring things.

But when I'm walking to the newsagent's, or travelling to a meeting, why do I need conscious thinking? What we usually call 'thinking' is really scattered ruminations of the 'monkey' mind, the mind chaotically and endlessly flitting from one scrap or image of sensation, desire or memory to another without any real purpose or effect. I might be worrying about whether I'll be late for the meeting, or wondering if there's some shopping that I can do nearby, or a sexual image may appear, or a wave of anxiety about work will just sway my consciousness and clutter my mind.

These are all distractions and take me away from what I really should be doing on my walk, which is simply – being aware of walking! It's enough for me to notice the sights and sounds of the streets I find myself in, the feel of my feet on the pavement, the smells around me, the warmth of the sun or the cool breeze on my face. I should just relax and enjoy all of this, since my brain will automatically and unconsciously make certain that my heart is beating, that I'll breathe enough oxygen (or what passes for it in my polluted city) to survive, and that I won't walk into a wall or fall into a hole in the ground. Instead of letting myself just enjoy existence, my conscious mind takes over and separates me from the sensual world that I inhabit.

If I really need to solve a problem, my brain will automatically focus on it and find the answer, but when there is no need to think, then mental chatter like this is just another way of taking us out of the world, losing our connection with primal existence.

Alan Watts, the Englishman who popularised Zen and Taoism in America, describes in his autobiography, *In My Own Way*, the defining moment when he first understood this point. He and his girlfriend were returning from a Buddhist meeting, and Alan was talking about his meditation method of concentrating on the eternal present. She said to him:

> *'Why try to concentrate on it? What else is there to be aware of? Your memories are all in the present, just as much as the trees over there. Your thoughts about the future are also in the present, and anyhow I just love to think about the future. The present is just a constant flow, like the Tao, and there's simply no way of getting out of it.'*

Watts says that this remark simply blew him away and he felt completely weightless. Infants live in this same weightless way, flowing with the present. A young child takes life as it comes, without the petty worries, discriminations and biased thoughts that adulthood puts in the way of that original pristine sense of existence. They don't have anxiety about the future, or fret over the past. They always live in the present, in the now, and they deal with life as it happens. It is the spontaneity of children that the Taoists value, because they consider the Tao as the source of pure spontaneity, and children operate naturally close to this ideal.

Unless stopped by adults, children live life to the full, whereas for most adults existence seems more of a near-life experience where we resemble actors rehearsing for a play that never quite begins, instead of playing fully, as children do, in a performance that has no beginning or end.

It's not just that children's behaviour is more natural than the conventional and inhibited behaviour of most grown-ups. The Taoists value spontaneity because they understand that this is a Law or Principle of Nature; it is in fact the Way of Nature, since flowers, insects, animals and the weather all exhibit complete spontaneity in action. Spontaneity is a core value of Taoism.

Yin and Yang

The *Tao Te Ching* sets out how the Tao spontaneously transforms itself from nothing into something, and how this spontaneity continues to produce the visible world:

> *The Tao gives birth to the One.*
> *The One gives birth to the Two.*
> *The Two gives birth to the Three –*
> *and the Three gives birth to every living thing.*

The Tao – chaotic, non-existent and formless – transforms into the One, the very first thing, which contains within it all the energy necessary to create a universe. The One is similar to what physicist Stephen Hawking calls a 'singularity', the pea-sized 'cosmic egg' whose explosion in the Big Bang began the expansion of our universe 15 billion years ago. This is the seed from which everything develops.

Having existence, the One contains Te (pronounced 'de') which is the inherent generative power that makes things happen. This is its Chinese character:

Te

The One inherits from the Tao energy, order, pattern and potential, all aspects of Te, which the One then provides to all of creation that evolves from it. The Taoists later portrayed the One like this:

The One

This state is open, undifferentiated, formless and chaotic like Tao but it has one difference – it exists in both time and space. After Tao transforms itself from Non-existence to Existence as the One, the One then divides into Two – the Tai Chi or supreme ultimate, the familiar Yin and Yang symbol:

Tai Chi

Taoism believes that everything else comes into existence from Yin and Yang acting together. Things are produced and then transformed by the operation of the two modes of Yin and Yang, where Yang represents the active, aggressive and expanding principle and Yin represents the passive, responsive and contracting principle.

Yang represents modes of positive and active force: movement, the sun, brightness, firmness, Heaven, masculine, hard, fire and heat, whilst Yin represents modes of negative and passive force: rest, the moon, dark, flexibility, Earth, feminine, soft, water and cold. Later, the Chinese differentiated everything possible into Yin and Yang modes, so that animals, food and even parts of the body are identified as Yin or Yang: the liver, heart, spleen, eyes and so on are Yang and the lungs, kidneys and mouth are Yin. These are their characters:

Yang

Yin

Yin and Yang represent a dynamic balance of forces in the natural world, a form of evening things out. Our aim in life is not to try to hold on to either one of these polar forces but to keep the two in balance. Yin and Yang forces are constantly trying to overwhelm each other, but in truth one cannot live without the other, and they are both mutually necessary.

The Tai Chi symbol shows that the universe is not static, but intensely alive and constantly changing through its cycles. Yin and Yang are eternally expanding and diminishing, and it's their mutual interaction that keeps the universe in movement.

It's in the nature of things that once Yang gets too powerful, it transforms into Yin and vice versa. This keeps the world's opposites from overwhelming each other, and maintains a natural form of harmony, a kind of natural justice.

Inside the brightness of Yang there's the black dot of Yin, and within the darkness of Yin there's the white dot of Yang. These two dots show that opposite forces grow and develop from within, maintaining an endless equilibrium between them. From this we recognise that masculine and feminine, for example, each share some characteristics of the other. The Taoist world is not one of rigid and absolute opposites, but involves the relativity of opposites, the complementarity of all characteristics.

For Chuang Tzu, the most important pair of Yin–Yang forces is Heaven (the Great Yang) and Earth (the Great Yin). Humanity is formed by the creative and active mode of Heaven working on the submissive and passive mode of Earth. We are therefore a mixture of Heaven and Earth, and in order to maintain harmony in our lives we need to find the right balance of the Heavenly and the Earthly. The follower of Tao only needs to imitate the actions of Heaven and Earth to become a sage or, to use Chuang Tzu's term, a Real Person of Tao.

Here are King Wan's explanations of the influences of Heaven and Earth from the *I Ching*, the ancient Chinese book of divination:

Heaven and Earth nourish all things. When Heaven moves and Earth rests, there follows production and transformation of everything.

Vast is the great and originating power of Heaven! It gives all things their beginning. The clouds move and rain is distributed, and the individual beings appear in their shapes.

Complete is the great and originating capacity of Earth! Being large and complete, it supports and contains all things. Its comprehension is wide, and its brightness is great! All things owe it their birth and through it obtain their full development. It obediently receives the influences of Heaven.

The method of Heaven is to move, change and transform, so that all creatures obtain their correct nature. Heaven diminishes the full and increases the empty. The method of Earth is to rest in its unlimited capacity, and it overthrows the full and replenishes the empty. Both of these preserve harmony in union.

Heaven's strength acts with ease, and Earth's stillness responds with simplicity.

One who attains the ease of Heaven will be easily understood, and one who attains the capacity of the simple will be easily followed. One who is easily understood will have followers, and one who is easily followed will achieve success. One who has followers can long endure, and one who has success can become great. To endure long shows the virtue of the wise and able. To become great is his acquired heritage.

Following the ease of Heaven and the simple freedom of Earth, one has mastery of all the principles of creation. With the attainment of that mastery, the sage makes good his position in the middle, between Heaven and Earth.

13

Te – Inner Power

We are made by the influences of Heaven and Earth, and contain within ourselves the qualities or characteristics of the Tao embedded in us as Te, our inner power: energy in the form of chi, order and pattern in our mind and body, and living potential in the form of our genes.

Tao functions through the power of Te, the force that lets our inherent potential qualities become realised and actualised throughout the experiences of life. As Chuang Tzu says, the Tao does nothing, and yet everything is produced. It is through the power of Te that the Tao produces everything.

To understand Te, consider that tree in the park. Like the universe, it starts from a tiny seed, and that seed contains its Te or potential. When that Te is actualised, through the natural forces of growth and development, the tree is brought to its full flowering, a mature and fully grown plant. Dylan Thomas's poem, *The Force That through the Green Fuse* poetically illustrates this:

> *The force that through the green fuse drives the flower,*
> *Drives my green age; that blasts the roots of trees*
> *Is my destroyer.*
> *And I am dumb to tell the crooked rose*
> *My youth is bent by the same wintry fever.*

The force that drives the water through the rocks
Drives my red blood; that dries the mouthing streams
Turns mine to wax.
And I am dumb to mouth unto my veins
How at the mountain spring the same mouth sucks.

Tao and the force of Te are in everything, both organic and non-organic, the living and the dead. Te is the force and potential that grows and develops a human being from a fertilised egg, and sustains that growth to maturity and beyond.

The film *Billy Elliot* shows an excellent example of Te. Young Billy, the eleven-year-old would-be dancer, is all unfulfilled potential, a potential inherent in his body and mind. When we see him at the end of the film, a ballet dancer in his prime, we see the full flowering of his Te, the potential that was in him now embodied in the vibrant and explosive leap that ends the film. Billy was lucky enough to be given a chance in life to realise his Te, when he could just as easily have been frustrated and denied.

In its full flowering, Te is also said to have a charismatic attraction, a mysterious magnetic quality that enables its possessor to influence other people solely through the force of realised character and personality, without having to exert physical force. This is the inner radiance of sages and all those who attract and motivate others.

Te also has the sense of being a kind of instant karma, in that each action we initiate has a consequence, sometimes immediate and sometimes delayed, but an inevitable effect follows, and our life is formed as a result of these individual actions. Consequently the *Tao Te Ching* cautions us that if we want to avoid the consequences of ill-considered actions, we need to act like the old sages:

Hesitant like one wading a stream in winter;
Timid like one afraid of his neighbours on all sides;

Cautious and courteous like a guest;
Yielding like ice on the point of melting;
Simple like an uncarved block;

To the Taoists, the aim of life, the art of living, is for each of us to have the freedom to realise our full Te, our inherent capacity to become a complete human being, and to fulfil that potential in the longest possible life. Chuang Tzu explains the process:

As things are completed, they have their distinct forms,
which we call shapes. Shape is the body preserving within it
the spirit, and each shape and spirit has its own innate nature.

When our nature has been properly cultivated,
it returns to its original and essential character.
When the original essence is recaptured,
there exists the same condition as at the very origin.

Our innate nature is perfect when we are infants, but we lose that perfection through conditioning, living the conventional life. The sage, the one who has found Tao, Chuang Tzu calls a Real Person because he's reversed this 'normal' process by cultivating his innate nature and restoring his original essence. His only concern is in retaining and perfecting his original spirit.

The Real Person does this through understanding what his real knowledge and capacity consist in:

The perfection of knowledge is to know what Heaven is,
and to know what the human is.
What is Heaven? That which gives life. What is human?
To know what we truly know and to nourish what we can't
know.
The perfection of knowledge is to enjoy one's natural life
and not die prematurely.

Taoism doesn't promise salvation or enlightenment. Salvation is part of the unknown and can't be relied on, and enlightenment as an end in itself is selfish. All Chuang Tzu wants is for us to live a full and enjoyable life. This doesn't seem like a very lofty or ambitious aim for a philosopher; it seems so easy and simple. Yet how many of us can manage it?

That's why the *Tao Te Ching* says:

> *My words are easy to understand,*
> *and very easy to practise.*
> *But no one in the world understands them,*
> *and no one practises them.*

What enables the sage, the Real Person, to do it? How has he or she managed to find the Tao?

14

Thawing the Ice

天

I've called chapter sixteen of the Book of Chuang Tzu 'The Seeker'; it tells the story of Nan Jung Chu, an older student of the Tao who joins Lao Tzu's school in order to find Tao. After ten days of self-cultivation, he's having a difficult time, and he asks Lao Tzu for something easy to practise:

> *'It is enough for me if you can just explain the Tao of keeping good health.'*

> Lao Tzu replied, *'You ask about keeping good health.*

> *'Can you embrace the One?*
> *Can you keep from losing it?*
> *Can you know good and bad fortune without consulting the oracle?*
> *Can you rest where you ought to rest?*
> *Can you stop when you have enough?*

> *'Can you leave others alone and seek it in yourself alone?*
> *Can you flee from desire?*
> *Can you be sincere?*
> *Can you become like a little child?*

> *'This is how to guard life.*

Nan Jung Chu said, 'And are these the characteristics of a Real Person?'

Lao Tzu replied, 'No. This is called thawing the ice, and melting the frost. Can you do it? The Real Person, along with others, shares food from Earth, and happiness from Heaven. But unlike others, he doesn't relate to considerations of profit and loss. Unlike others, he doesn't do strange things, form plans, or have projects. He flees the allure of desire, and pursues his way with a complete simplicity.

'This is the way he guards his life.'

We are born with what the Taoists call the Mind of Tao, but the conditioning of society distorts it and replaces it with the Human Mind. Taoists believe that before we can resurrect this hidden Mind of Tao, we need to go into a process of Thawing, a de-conditioning of the ideas we already consciously and unconsciously hold. We need to learn how to look at the world not as a world of opposites (pleasure and pain, wealth and poverty, health and disease) of which we must always pursue one and deny the other as strenuously as possible, but to look on it as a whole, a unity of which the opposites are only polar manifestations of Yin and Yang.

The Mind of Tao is not analytical. Instead it operates or functions like the Tao itself: it doesn't discriminate, doesn't take sides, but allows things to happen spontaneously, without interfering. It tries to hold opposites together, and see what it is they hold in common. It doesn't immediately need to take sides, decide on what it likes and dislikes and rush off in pursuit, but it examines both views in a synthesis and patiently waits to see what develops. It is a state of complete openness.

This way of acting without acting, of not interfering, is called wu-wei, and has been translated as non-striving, not trying, or doing nothing. This is its character:

wu-wei

But wu wei is far from doing nothing. It really means not forcing things, being willing to watch as things develop naturally by themselves before making a move, rather than jumping in anxiously and disturbing them.

The Real Person uses doing nothing as a guide to action, being careful not to be too early or too late, but to move 'just in time'. Often this move is seen as an inevitability, when there is no other choice. But inevitability is just the reverse side of the coin of spontaneity. The Real Person models his actions on Heaven and Earth, which 'do' nothing but create everything, in a way that is simultaneously spontaneous and inevitable. Chuang Tzu explains:

I consider 'doing nothing' to be the greatest happiness, while ordinarily people consider 'doing nothing' to be a great evil. Hence it is paradoxically said, 'Perfect happiness is to be without happiness; the highest praise is to be without praise.'

The right or wrong of this point of happiness can't be determined according to the view of the world. Nevertheless, 'doing nothing' or 'not trying' to obtain happiness can actually judge both the right and the wrong. Since we consider perfect happiness to be in keeping oneself alive, it's only by 'doing nothing' that this can be achieved.

I'll try to explain this a bit more:
Heaven does nothing, and so maintains its serenity.
Earth does nothing, and so has its peace.
By the union of these two non-active forces, everything is
    produced.
How vast and imperceptible is this process!
Things seem to come from nowhere!
How imperceptible and vast!
We can't begin to see it!

All things in all their variety grow from this inaction.
Hence the saying, 'Heaven and Earth do nothing, and yet
there is nothing that remains undone.'
But can we find anyone who trusts the universe enough to live
according to 'doing nothing'?

The Real Person trusts the universe enough to allow it to dictate what happens, and he doesn't try to force the world to fulfil his demands. When we die, we all return to our original state of emptiness and rejoin Tao. But the Real Person, because he imitates the actions of Tao and trusts in it, is able to return to the emptiness of Tao even while alive. By learning how to return while still alive, and watch for the inevitable return of everything else, he's able to partake of the power of the Tao in his daily life.

This is what the *Tao Te Ching* means when it says:

Attaining utter emptiness,
maintaining single-minded stillness,
as things act together,
I thereby watch their return.

By maintaining emptiness, the Real Person trusts that Heaven and Earth will fill him, as King Wen had described:

Heaven diminishes the full and increases the empty.
Earth overthrows the full and replenishes the empty.

It's the eternal cyclical action of Yin and Yang that fills and empties, empties and fills.

The Real Person has learned to retain his original mind and he uses it like a perfect mirror. It reflects everything perfectly, but doesn't hold on to anything. Consider a still lake high up in the mountains on a clear day, its surface unruffled by wind or rain. The placid water is like a mirror, reflecting all the birds and clouds that pass overhead. When birds fly by, they appear on the surface, and when they sail on, their image dissolves. The lake has no desire to reflect the clouds, but can't help doing it. And since it has no desire to retain the images, returns again to pristine purity.

To make the mind a perfect mirror is to use the Mind of Tao rather than the Human Mind. But this requires more than a little discipline and training. Because once we decide that such a mind is worth attaining, we need to start work on polishing and repairing the mind that we already possess. To correct our distorted and even partly opaque mirror is to start a process of transformation of consciousness, a daunting and sometimes difficult task.

The Human Mind is the conscious mind concerned with worldly things and worldly life. It's a rational and objective mind that looks at life and makes distinctions and discriminations about what it sees. But these discriminations are based on our desires, and in particular on the desire to seek pleasure and to avoid pain. So our likes and dislikes, the things we want to pursue and the things we want to avoid, make up the bulk of the Human Mind's activities, and this mind is dead certain that its analysis is correct.

Our Human Mind looks on life and sees that it's short and temporary, that it's insecure, full of fears and problems and that it all ends in death. It sees that life seems to be based on chance and has little or no meaning. As Thomas Hobbes said, 'Life is nasty, brutish, and short.' Based on that premise, it sets out a method for coping with such an existence.

Since life is short it must be clung to by any means, and we must pursue every possible way to extend that short term. Since it's insecure, we must always seek security, which money, property and possessions seem to provide. Since life is temporary and death inevitable, we must seek out fame and honour so that our passing has some meaning, and we need to leave behind children and memorials to keep our name alive, beyond physical death.

Though death is inevitable, we try to deny it, and cling to beliefs that convince us that though our bodies die our souls can be immortal. We seek health to prolong life, but are willing to abandon health for the sake of dangerous pleasures like smoking, excessive drinking and other harmful drugs. The contradictory nature of the Human Mind means that it inevitably comes into conflict with itself, and its see-saw effect of living on the emotions of hope and fear leads us to the heights of joy before plunging us down again to depths of despair.

It is only partly our fault that we make this Human Mind for ourselves. It's mainly given to us by society, by the opinions and ideas of our parents, friends, teachers and the media. Our Human Mind has been a very long time in construction, having come down to us through the experiences of all our ancestors. But it's our parents who are given the job of forming its early conditioning and who instil in us the basic ideas of life that we then apply unconsciously in our own experience.

Chuang Tzu and the Taoists believe that the conventional, obvious and well-trodden ways are often the most delusive. If we always live in imitation of other people, we may be following a way that is completely wrong for us, and so may never live a way that feels right. It's so easy to lose yourself by following patterns set by others.

Taoism wants us to become the creator of our own lives, as if we are sculptors who are given a mass of clay and the freedom to form the most natural and therefore best version of our self. Many of us would like to have a chance to remake what has already been made, and perhaps made badly, by the ideas and people that originally formed us.

This creative approach to transformation is empowering, because it enables us to examine our problems and pains, understand them, and see what changes need to take place in our minds and bodies in order to discover our real and original self, our innate nature, what the Buddhists call 'our original face', ideally without these old acquired flaws.

Many difficulties we experience stem from our own false judgements about the world. We make these judgements in ignorance or through self-seeking, so that, in effect, we create our own problems and difficulties. The judgements, decisions and opinions we have about the world are dependent on the state of our minds. If we can change the way we think we can literally change the way we see the world, and our experiences will consequently be different.

Although it's easy for me to say, 'Change your mind and the world you experience will itself change', it's quite another thing to put such changes into effect. We're creatures of habit, and we've been conditioned to see the world in a certain way. Not only that, our bodies have also become conditioned, and hold in our cells and muscles many old and harmful habits of posture and use. To change that conditioning is a very deep-seated matter of altering one's lifestyle, personality and character, no easy task.

But we need to see the world clearly, not coloured by our desires, or the short-term needs of our limited self. Most of the time we look at life through this limited ego, and we make decisions and judgements based on what we assume we need to be happy.

To make correct judgements we need to know what we

really think and feel about things, and not what others who have influenced us thought about them. In particular, we need to be certain that we are able to tell the difference between the real and the artificial, the true and the false, because without this one primary distinction we're unable to make any correct judgements at all. To be able to discriminate between the real and the artificial is the beginning of wisdom; it's the only way to lose ignorance and gain understanding.

The Mind of Tao is a perfect mirror. It sees everything that comes in front of it in the greatest clarity of detail. It can't be fooled by illusion. And when an object is taken away, the mirror doesn't retain the image, but it fades completely from view.

The Human Mind doesn't act like this. It sees the world through a mirror of bias and distortion, a reflection altered by desire, which creates images that aren't clear, but twisted and prejudiced by emotion. And when these images disappear, the Human Mind tries to hold on to them, either in memory, or by actively gazing out in yearning from the mirror itself, seeking positive attachment.

If we can de-condition our minds, thaw our fixed and frozen ideas of conventional reality and bring out that hidden mind of Tao, using it like a perfect mirror, then we're acting like Chuang Tzu's Real People:

The sage is entirely peaceful, so his mind is evenly balanced and at ease. This even balance and ease appears in his serenity and detachment. In this state of balance and ease, of serenity and detachment, anxieties and anguish don't affect him, and no harmful influences assault him. His Te, or power, is complete, and his spirit continues undiminished.

The sage responds to the influences acting on him, and moves only when he feels the pressure. He acts only when he has no

66

other choice. He discards knowledge and memories, and merely follows the pattern of his Heaven-given nature. Therefore he suffers no calamity from Heaven, no attachment to things, no blame from people, and no disapproval from the spirits of the dead.

The sage's life seems to just drift along;
his death seems to be a resting;
he doesn't have anxious thoughts;
he doesn't make plans;
his enlightenment is hidden;
his good faith isn't contrived;
he sleeps untroubled by dreams;
he wakes untroubled by cares;
his spirit is simple and pure;
his soul is never weary.

Empty and selfless, calm and detached, the sage is in harmony with the virtue of Heaven.

By acting like this, we no longer interpose our conscious mind between Tao flowing in the universe at large and Tao flowing in ourselves. We get out of the way of the stronger and more primal force, and let go, letting it act naturally through us. Keeping a unity between Tao inside and Tao outside, Tao flows simply and easily with us in all of life's activities.

To follow Tao is to live a life in which happiness, serenity and satisfaction are not just the result of moments of directed pleasure or of hope fulfilled, but can be a steady stream of pleasurable and fulfilling experiences throughout the various parts of life: work, play, parenting, relationships, sexuality and spirituality, art and religion, music and wine. A life in touch and flowing with the original essence of existence can restore us to the wholeness that we seek, and which seems impossible to find through conventional means.

The Taoists believed that the Real Person could eventually become an 'immortal', because he or she had found the hidden secret of creation, and used that secret in their own life, reversing the effects of mundane desires and finding instead a fulfilment of potential undreamed of in ordinary existence. Chuang Tzu describes the 'immortal' in these extravagant and fantastic terms:

> *Far away on Mount Ku lives a man of spirit. His skin is smooth like ice and white as snow. His manners are as shy and delicate as a young girl's. He doesn't eat the fruits of the earth, but inhales the wind and drinks the dew.*
> *He ascends on clouds of chi, and drives flying dragons, rambling and enjoying himself beyond the four seas. By concentrating his spirit he protects people from disease and decay, and ensures a plentiful harvest.*

Because we live in a sceptical and prosaic society we doubt whether it's possible for anyone to become an immortal and fly on the wind. But it's other doubts, more basic and deepseated, that stop us from pursuing a path like Taoism, or indeed any spiritual path at all.

Doubt is the main problem in discovering the Mind of Tao and putting its light into practice. Unlike the Real Person of Tao, most of us have lost trust, both in ourselves and in the universe, and have allowed doubt to take the place trust used to inhabit. It wasn't always so.

15

Trust Dr Müller

In his book *The Varieties of Religious Experience*, William James discusses a Victorian minister, George Müller of Bristol, who died in 1898. Müller had resolved early in his life to take on trust certain biblical promises literally, and to let himself be fed, not by his own foresight, but by the hand of God.

This led to an extraordinarily productive career in which he distributed two million copies of the Bible, equipped several hundred missionaries, circulated over 100 million tracts and pamphlets, built and kept up five large orphanages, and established schools in which 120,000 pupils were taught. In the course of his work Müller received and administered nearly £1.5 million (£70 million in today's currency) and travelled 200,000 miles over land and sea, at a time when there were no airplanes or cars.

During the sixty-eight years of his ministry, he never owned any property except his clothes and furniture, and when he died at eighty-six, he left an estate worth only £160.

Müller was a devout Christian who believed and trusted in the power of God. A book about Müller's activities called *The Life Of Trust* said:

> *His method was to let his general needs be publicly known, but not to acquaint other people with the details of his temporary*

necessities. For the relief of these, he prayed directly to the Lord, believing that sooner or later prayers are always answered if one has enough trust. Müller wrote, 'When I lose such a thing as a key, I ask the Lord to direct me to it, and I look for an answer to my prayer; when I do not understand a passage of the word of God, I lift up my heart to the Lord that he would be pleased by his Holy Spirit to instruct me, and I expect to be taught, though I do not fix the time when, and the manner how it should be.'

The 'necessaries' Müller mentions were the food and fuel of his orphanages. Somehow, near as they often came to going without a meal, they hardly ever seem to have done so.

'Greater and more manifest nearness of the Lord's presence I have never had than when after breakfast there were no means for dinner for more than a hundred persons; or when after dinner there were no means for the tea, and yet the LORD provided the tea; and all this without one single human being having been informed of our need. . . Through Grace my mind is so fully assured of the faithfulness of the Lord, that in the midst of the greatest need, I am enabled in peace to go about my other work.'

Müller had complete trust in God and believed that God heard his prayers and answered them. But what if we don't believe in a personal God who listens to us and answers us? What if we believe God exists but doesn't care about us? What then can we find to believe in? Can we somehow find the kind of trust that gave Müller the confidence to undertake the impossible and pull it off? If so, what is it that we can trust?

For the last 5,000 years trust in the universe for Jews and Christians involved a belief in a providential and ever-watchful God, a father-protector who looked after us and didn't forget us or abandon us. As Yahweh (God) said in the Sinai desert to Moses, 'I will be there, and my word will be your helper.' But in the West, in the twenty-first century, most people no longer believe that God's presence is still here. We feel abandoned, and have lost the complete trust in God that our relatives felt only a few generations ago.

Even those who still believe in God lack the kind of trust that Dr Müller exhibited. In the past two years I've attended two conferences where Rabbi Jesus's teachings on the parable of the lilies of the field was mentioned. This teaching is remarkably close in spirit to the Taoist wu wei – doing nothing:

> *Therefore I tell you, don't take thought for your own life – what you will eat, or for your body – what you will wear. Isn't your life more than its food and your body more than its clothing? Consider the birds in the sky. They don't sow or harvest or collect for granaries, yet your Heavenly Father feeds them. And aren't you preferred to them?*
>
> *Which of you by thinking can add one inch to his height? Why worry about clothes? Consider the lilies of the field, how they grow. They don't till fields or spin cloth, yet I tell you not even Solomon in all his glory was adorned like them. And if God clothes the grass of the field, which grows today and tomorrow is cut down, how much more will He clothe you, you of little faith? Don't fret and say: What shall we eat and drink? What shall we wear? Let the Gentiles worry about that. Your Father in Heaven knows you need these things. But first seek out His kingdom and His justice, then all things will be given to you. Don't worry about tomorrow, tomorrow will take care of itself, for every day has more than enough of its own evil.*

On each occasion the speaker declared that neither he, nor anyone he knew, could live according to this precept. And on each occasion the audience had a good laugh at this remark. I wondered what it was that brought on the laughter.

Their laughter said, 'How can Jesus expect us to live like this? It's so unrealistic. We will be poor; we will starve; we won't have homes; we won't survive.' What their laughter exposed wasn't their faith in Christianity but their doubts about it. This is a key teaching of Christianity, yet in audiences largely made up of Christians, it was clear that almost no one believed in this teaching or could even imagine applying it in their lives.

By not having trust in the power of the universe, which is the same as the power of Tao, we're unable to follow it and so fail to benefit from its power. The power of the universe is Yang, it is strength itself. By not trusting this strength we fall back, for security, on our own limited power. We think we have no alternative but to rely only on ourselves. But this is the Yin of self, it's not real strength, but is its opposite – weakness. We fail to trust the strength of the universe, and instead push forward our own strength, but deep down we don't really believe in it, because we know that over time it will fail us – will diminish and depart.

The *Tao Te Ching* knows all about the laughter I heard:

When the wise student hears about Tao,
he practises diligently.

When the average student hears about Tao,
he wavers between belief and doubt.

And when poor students hear about it,
they have a good laugh!

But if they didn't laugh at it,
it wouldn't be Tao!

Doubt, scepticism, and cynicism have gradually replaced trust, and we've discovered that these feelings don't appear alone, but have fellow travellers that accompany them, in an increasing sense of fear and anxiety, even anguish. These negative attitudes have led to a corresponding and increasing deadening of feelings and a hardening of the heart. This makes for a kind of emptiness too, but it's not the emptiness of the Real Person, who's waiting to be filled with the living potential of the Tao. This is the dead end of emptiness – nihilism.

Trust in the universe meant trust in God, but without God to believe in, we are now searching, some of us consciously, and I believe the rest of us unconsciously, for something else to believe in. Because without trust in something, we can only spiral further down the path of an alienated, heartless and cold society, dedicated to satisfying only selfish material needs, and in the process destroying the only home we have, our beautiful green Earth.

If you can't trust that the universe will, in its own way, look after you and protect you, like the lilies of the field, it means that you have no trust in yourself, since ultimately, as my daughter understood, we are each, in a real sense, our own universe. If you're full of doubts and fears about life, these are really doubts and fears you hold about yourself. Since what we give out returns to us, the world reflects what we hold in our hearts. Without God, is there anything in the universe or its creation that gives meaning and purpose to life?

Scientists and Taoists agree that the universe is a spontaneous creation out of nothing. What is especially striking is that it was created on a critical razor's edge of possibility. That is, the universe expanded under conditions (gravitation, electricity, the weak and strong nuclear reactions) that were so finely tuned and so delicately poised that the tiniest increase or decrease of forces would have destroyed it.

A minuscule increase would have led to an open universe that would have expanded too fast to sustain life and the tiniest decrease to a closed one that would have collapsed in on itself. The creation and survival of our universe have to be seen as not just unlikely and improbable but truly miraculous and mysterious.

Given that the creation of the universe was so critical and precarious, and therefore special, and that the eventual birth of a green planet capable of sustaining life is, as far as we know, also unique, it isn't surprising that the magic of life generated in our ancestors a state of wonder and awe, natural religious feelings. The ancient Celts, Jews, Greeks, Egyptians, Indians, Chinese and others recognised how astounding it was to be alive and they celebrated this in their art, poetry and rituals.

But we, who have discovered and proved the laws of nature that explain all this, and who intellectually and objectively understand how truly remarkable it is that we even exist, have so little spirituality or poetry left in our souls to celebrate it.

So many of us take life more or less for granted, have lost a sense of gratitude for the simple pleasures of existence, until illness or some other disaster wakes us up to what we are and have. Until that time, we have little sense of wonder, reverence or respect to reflect that the conditions that created us are so, in a word, miraculous. We have lost many of the traditional means of celebrating life, of recognising and praising a power greater than our own. This lack of feeling about the world and our existence shows the deadening of our contemporary souls. It's no wonder that we are polluting and destroying the Earth with so little sense of shame.

The Taoists understood how amazing it was to be alive, as the *Tao Te Ching* reflects:

> *Does anyone want to take the world and do what he wants*
> *   with it?*
> *I don't see how he can succeed.*

> *The Earth is a sacred vessel, which mustn't be tampered with*
> *or grabbed after.*
> *To tamper with it is to spoil it, and to grasp after it is to lose*
> *it.*

The Earth is sacred. The Taoists understood intuitively that not only did Hawking's 'singularity' contain all the matter in the universe, but it must also have contained all the non-matter, or spirit. Otherwise how do we account for the existence of mind and consciousness? For them, Tao is the source of everything, and everything includes spirit, and in particular the human spirit. The human spirit is where we truly live, and where, if we look, we can find the answers to the anxieties and doubts that now assail us. But to liberate our human spirit we first need to acknowledge that it exists, and not be afraid of the feelings associated with it.

> *Now, the person who possesses the finest sword preserves it*
> *carefully in a box, and doesn't dare to use it, because it's con-*
> *sidered the peak of perfection. But the subtle human spirit is*
> *even more perfect, and it radiates in all directions, flowing on*
> *without limit, rising to Heaven above, and circling round the*
> *Earth beneath. It transforms and sustains all things, and*
> *can't be represented by any form. We call it the Supreme*
> *Harmony.*

Can the problems and anxieties we associate with contemporary life be solved by an ancient practice like Taoism? We have to understand that the primary problems we face are, in essence, no different from the experiences and difficulties mankind has faced for the past 2,500 years, since making that giant leap into self-awareness.

The experiences of a twenty-first century office worker, residing in a city, and living almost totally dependent on a proliferating technology, may be diametrically opposed to that of an ancient Chinese farmer, living on a smallholding in a 'primitive' agricultural society, but the relationships that count in life, the inner relationships that give meaning to our existence, are both few and enduring. They have never changed.

To paraphrase both Bob Marley and the Jewish theologian Martin Buber, the relations that matter are only three: those of 'I and I', 'I and You' and 'I and It'. What is essential is that these three relationships all remain in balance and that the feelings engendered by them are all of a piece. We need our inner and outer lives to be completely harmonious, and to achieve that state our relationship with ourself – I and I, our relationships with other people – I and You, and our relationship to the universe – I and It, must not be contradictory and divisive. For when we are divided and fight against ourselves we, and all those close to us, are the only losers.

The ancient sages understood that the good life needed to be more than just survival, that perfect health and many years to enjoy it was as real a satisfaction as could be found, and that the conventional desires that have driven humanity for so long – the big three of money, power and status – were in the end illusions that attached, bound and enslaved rather than liberated. Commodities, the things of the world, are necessary for survival, but the freedom of the human spirit is the only value really worth pursuing.

I've been attracted to Taoism because the philosophy and practices of this ancient teaching have shown me that it's possible to change one's entire way of looking at the world without having to leave the world. Some philosophies and religions seem to work if we're prepared to become celibate monks, or live in retreats, or seclude ourselves with people who share the same creed and values, or live in an artificially 'spiritual' way. But Taoism is a philosophy that's designed for daily life, for the life of the kitchen, the bed, the school and the marketplace.

It's transcendental, in that it believes there is something spiritual in life, and this spiritual quality is most important and nourishing, but it also says that spirit isn't separate from everyday life, from the daily activities of minds and bodies.

Taoism finds a way to integrate the differing aspects of mind and body, while at the same time appreciating and celebrating the qualities of each. Taoism is the great harmoniser of differences, giving mind and body an equality, and allowing them to synthesise together and operate holistically, as nature intended.

QUEENS PARK, LONDON
January 2001

A Note On The Text

The *Book of Chuang Tzu* has come down to us in thirty-three chapters, of which the first seven are known as the Inner Chapters and are considered the actual work of Chuang Tzu. The remaining chapters are a mixture, some from the school of Chuang Tzu, some sections possibly by the master himself, and other chapters from different branches of Taoism. Some of these outer chapters are much later than Chuang Tzu, possibly down to the third century CE (Christian era).

The Inner Chapters, the work of the Master himself, are of much higher quality than almost all the other material. From the original thirty-three chapters, I've made a selection of the most interesting and best-written texts. Some of these I've shortened, one or two I've merged, but most are left in their complete form. This selection comprises about half of the original book. I've placed the texts into new thematic chapters, sixteen in all, and put them in what I hope is an interesting and sensible order.

The main English translation I worked from is that of James Legge, from 1891, and I consulted a number of more contemporary translations, to clarify certain ideas and issues. Of these newer translations, I was particularly helped by *The Book of Chuang Tzu* by Martin Palmer and Elizabeth Breuilly, *Chuang Tsu Inner Chapters* by Gia-Fu Feng and Jane English, *Wandering on the Way* by Victor H. Mair, *Chuang Tzu* by Burton Watson, and *A Taoist Classic Chuang Tzu* by Fung Yu-Lan.

PART TWO

The Book of
Chuang Tzu

CHAPTER ONE

Finding the Tao

The Tao Is Everywhere

Tung Kuo Tzu asked Chuang Tzu, 'Where can I find this thing you call the Tao?'

'It's everywhere,' said Chuang Tzu.

Tung said, 'Give me an example – that will be easier.'

'It's here in this ant,' pointed Chuang Tzu.

'That's a bit low, isn't it?'

'It's also in the grass.'

'Does it go any lower?'

'It's in these shards of tile.'

'I suppose that's the lowest example?'

'Not really – it's also in this dog turd.'

Tung Kuo Tzu was lost for words.

Chuang Tzu said, 'Your questions miss the fundamental point of Tao.

'When the Superintendent of Markets was asked why he put his foot on the pigs, he explained that the deeper his foot sank, the fatter the pig.

'Like the Superintendent, there's no need to be too specific, because there's no single thing that exists without Tao. It's the same with the Perfect Tao. And if I choose to call it Great Tao it's still just the same. There are these three words: "complete" – "all-embracing" – "universal". These words are all different, but the reality sought in them is the same, and refers to wholeness, unity, the One.

'Suppose you and I were to wander together in the land of Nowhere. There, we could discuss this subject endlessly. Or suppose we were together in the region of Doing Nothing. How quiet and peaceful we would be! How simple and pure! How relaxed and harmonious!

'Our wills would be completely aimless. We would wander off, but not know where we'd gone. We might go and return, and not know where we'd stopped. Going and coming, going and returning, we wouldn't know when it might end, roaming in the vastness of space. Though I entered it with the greatest knowledge, I would never discover how inexhaustible it was.

'The power that makes things what they are doesn't have the limitation that belongs to things, and when we speak of things being limited, we mean that they're bounded in themselves. The Tao is the limit of the unlimited, and the boundlessness of the unbounded.

'We speak of fullness and emptiness, of withering and decay. The Tao produces this fullness and emptiness, but is itself neither full nor empty. It produces withering and decay, but will never itself wither or decay. It produces the roots and branches, but is neither root nor branch. It gathers together and it disperses, but is itself neither gathered nor dispersed.'

Confucius Seeks Tao

Confucius was fifty-one years old and had still not attained the Tao, so he went south to see Lao Tzu, who said to him, 'So you've come, Sir? I've heard that you're the wisest man in the north. Haven't you found Tao yet?'

'Not yet,' admitted Confucius.

The old man went on, 'How have you looked for it?'

Confucius said, 'At first I looked for it in what can be measured and counted, but after five years I didn't find it.'

'Then what did you do?'

'I looked for it in Yin and Yang, and after twelve years I still haven't found it.'

Lao Tzu said, 'That's right! If Tao could be presented to another, people would all present it to their rulers. If it could be served to others, people would all serve it to their parents. If it could be told to others, people would tell it to their brothers and sisters. If it could be given to others, people would all give it to their sons and daughters.

'There are reasons why it can't be transmitted. If, inside, there's no true centre, Tao will not stay. And if, outside, there's no true acquiescence, Tao will not be carried out.

'When that which flows from the mind in possession of the Tao isn't received by the minds receiving it, the sage won't give it out. And if, when Tao enters in from outside, there's no true centre to welcome it, the sage won't allow it to lie hidden there.

'Fame is a possession common to everyone, so we should-n't desire to have too much of it. Goodness and justice are like lodging houses of the former kings, useful to rest in for only one night, and not for an extended stay. If people see us doing so, they will have much to say against us.

'The Real People of old walked the Tao of goodness as a path which they borrowed for the occasion, and dwelt in justice as a lodging which they used for just a night. In this way they rambled carefree in the empty void, found their food in the open fields, and enjoyed gardens which weren't theirs. Emptiness requires us to do nothing, indifference is easily supplied with nourishment, and not borrowing needs no outlay. The ancients called this 'rambling free to collect the Real.'

'Those who think wealth the most important thing can't give up their revenue. Those who seek distinction can't live without desiring fame. Those who cleave to power can't hand it over to others. While they grasp these things, they live in fear of losing them, and become miserable when they do. They refuse to look at a single example which might show them the folly of their restless ways. Such people suffer the punishment of Heaven.

'Hatred and kindness, taking and giving, correction and instruction, death and life. These eight things are tools for regeneration, but only those who are willing to adapt to great changes are able to use them. Hence it is said, "Correction is Regeneration." If their hearts don't acknowledge this, it's because their Heavenly gate hasn't yet opened.'

Pursue the Tao of Nature

There's a limit to life, but to knowledge there's no limit. Using what's limited to seek out the unlimited is futile. And if, knowing this, we still act according to knowledge, then danger can't be avoided.

Don't do good for the sake of gain, and if you pursue evil then try not to get punished. To be in accord with the Tao of your own nature is the regular way to preserve your body, to maintain life, to nourish your inner core, and to live out your years.

What is this Tao of our own nature? I'll tell you some stories that illuminate it.

The Wood Carver

Ching, the woodcarver, was known as the king of wood.

Once he carved a bell-stand for the Court of Lu, and when it was completed, everyone who gazed at it was astonished, thinking it had to be the work of gods or spirits. The Marquis of Lu went to see it, and asked Ching what art he had used in making it.

'I'm only a craftsman,' said Ching. 'What "art" should I possess? Nevertheless there is something I can mention. When I had undertaken to make the bell-stand I didn't want to waste any of my chi, my vital energy, so I felt it necessary to fast in order to concentrate my mind.

'After fasting for three days, I no longer thought of congratulations, rewards, rank or money which I might gain. After fasting for five days, I no longer thought of any praise or blame that this work might produce, or of the skill or lack of skill that it might display. At the end of the seventh day of fasting, I was so still that I had forgotten myself completely: my four limbs and my whole body. By this time the thought of Your Grace's court had dissolved completely. My mind was concentrated exclusively on the exercise of my skill.

'Then I wandered into the forest, and looked at the natural forms of the trees. When I found one of perfect form, the image of the bell-stand presented itself to my mind, and I knew that with this tree I could apply my hand to the work. Had I not found this tree, I would have abandoned the job. But my Heaven-given skill and the Heaven-given qualities of the wood harmonised perfectly, and perhaps this is the reason people think the bell-stand was made by spirits.'

Concentration

One day Confucius saw a hunchback catching cicadas on the point of a sticky pole, catching them as easily as if he were picking them up with his hand! He watched in amazement. 'You are very clever at this,' said Confucius. 'Do you have Tao?'

The hunchback replied, 'I do. For six months I practised balancing two balls until they didn't fall, and after that I caught a small fraction of the cicadas. Then I practised with three balls and could manage one cicada in ten. Finally, after training with five balls, I caught the cicadas as if I were gathering them in.

'When I do this, I regard my body as nothing more than the stump of a broken tree, and my shoulder as no more than a rotten branch. Heaven and Earth are great, and there's a dizzying abundance of things in the world, but I take no notice of any of them, and concentrate my entire being on the tiny wings of my cicadas. I wouldn't exchange those wings for all the wealth in the world – how then could I fail to catch them?'

Confucius turned, and said to his students, 'The ancients say, "Where the will is undivided, the spirit is concentrated".' They could have been speaking of this hunchbacked gentleman.'

Complete Spirit

Chi Hsing Tzu was training a fighting cock for the King.

After ten days he was asked if the bird was ready, and he said, 'Not yet. He's still vain and quarrelsome, and relies on his own spirit.'

After another ten days, he said, 'He isn't ready yet. He's still alarmed by the appearance of another bird.'

After ten days more, he replied, 'No, Not yet. He still looks fiercely, and is full of spirit.'

When the fortieth day had passed, he replied to the question, 'Nearly ready. Though another cock crows, he doesn't react in the slightest. To look at him, you would say he was a cock made of wood. His inner quality is now complete. He has no need to fight, because no other cock will dare to confront him.'

Losing Oneself in the Water

Confucius was visiting the waterfall near the gorge of Lu. The cataract falls from a dizzy height, its spray floating over the surrounding country, producing a wild turbulence in the river below, in which no fish can swim.

Looking at the billowing white water he was amazed to see an old man tossed around by the waves, and wondered if he'd sustained a great tragedy, and wanted to end his life. Confucius urged his students to rescue him, but by the time they got to the water, the old man was walking along singing, his white hair wet and dishevelled, relaxing at the foot of the embankment.

Confucius approached him, and said, 'To survive that fall I thought you must have been a ghost. But when I look closely, I see that you really are a man. Can I ask if you have any particular Tao of dealing with the water.'

The man said, 'No, I have no particular Tao. I began to learn this skill when I was very young. As I grew up, it became my nature to practise, and my success is now as sure as destiny. I plunge into the water and get swept by it to the very centre of its whirl, and am thrown up again with it when it whirls the other way. I just let my watery nature go along with the Tao of the water, and don't attempt to oppose it. This is how I do it.'

Confucius said, 'What do you mean by saying that you began to learn the skill when you were very young, that as you grew up, it became your nature to practise, and that your success in it now is as sure as destiny?'

The man replied, 'I was born among these hills and lived contentedly here. That's why I say I've been nurtured by this water from infancy. I grew up with it, and felt secure swimming in it; that's why I said that to flow with it had become natural to me. I have no idea how I do it, and yet I do it. That's why I say that my success is as sure as destiny.'

Forgetting the Dangers

Yen Yuan asked Confucius, 'When I was crossing the gorge at Chang Shan, the ferryman handled the boat like a spirit. I asked him whether handling a boat like that could be learned, and he replied, "It may. Good swimmers can learn it quickly, and divers, even if they've never seen a boat, can manage it at once." Can you explain what he meant?'

Confucius replied, 'Good swimmers learn the ability quickly because they ignore the water and its dangers. As for those who know how to dive and, without ever having seen a boat, can manage it at once, they regard the sea as if it was a hillside, and a capsizing boat like a carriage reversing. These upsets and reverses have happened to them innumerable times, and have never seriously disturbed their minds. Wherever they go, they feel at ease with what happens to them.

'In an archery competition, if the prize is a certificate, an archer will be uninhibited and use all his skill. But if the prize is a silver cup, he may become hesitant. And when the prize is a golden statue, he might shoot as if he were blind. The archer's skill is the same all three times, but in the two latter cases he's affected by his nerves and magnifies the importance of the prize. To attach too much importance to external things makes you careless about internal ones.'

Lessons from the Chef

King Hui's cook was carving an ox. When he placed his hand, leaned forward with his shoulder, planted his foot, and thrust his knee, in the audible tearing of the ox's skin and the slicing of the knife, the sounds were all in a distinct rhythm. It was almost as if the cook were performing a dance.

King Hui looked on in admiration and said, 'I am amazed at the perfection of your skill!'

The cook laid down his knife and replied, 'What your servant loves is the method of Tao, something which is far in advance of any skill. When I first learned to cut up an ox, what I saw was the entire carcass. After three years I ceased to see it as a whole. Now I deal with it through my spirit alone, and have no need to look at it with my eyes. My senses stop functioning and I follow only my spirit.

'Observing the natural lines of the ox, my knife slips through the great crevices and slides through the hidden openings, taking advantage of what is there. Thus I avoid the tough sinews, and even more the massive bones.

'An ordinary cook changes his knife every month, because he hacks with it. A good cook only changes his every year, because in cutting it gets damaged. Now my knife has been in use for nineteen years, and it's cut up several thousand oxen, and yet its edge is as sharp as if it had just come from the grindstone.

'There are the dense inner linings of the joints, and the blade of my knife has no appreciable thickness. When that which is so thin enters where the lining is, how smoothly it glides along! The blade has more than enough room.

'Nevertheless, when I come to a complicated joint, and see that there may be some difficulty, I proceed carefully and with caution, not allowing my eyes to leave the spot, and slowly slide my hand. Finally, with a slight twist of my knife, the flesh is quickly separated, and drops like a clod of earth to the ground.

'Then, standing with the knife in my hand, I look all around, and in a leisurely manner, with a feeling of satisfaction, I wipe it clean, and put it in its sheath.'

King Hui said, 'Well done! I've heard the words of my cook, and from him have learned how to nourish life.'

Dregs

The world thinks the most valuable exhibition of Tao is found in its classic books. But books are only a collection of words. Words are valuable: what is valuable in them is the ideas they convey. But those ideas are a sequence of something else, and that something else can't be conveyed by words.

When the world, because of the high value it attaches to words, commits those words to books, the thing it so values them for may not deserve to be valued. Because what the world values isn't really what's valuable.

That's why what we look at and see is only the outward form and colour, and what we listen to and hear are only names and sounds. How sad that people should think that form and colour, name and sound, are enough to give them the real nature of Tao!

Form and colour, name and sound, are certainly not sufficient to convey its real nature, and that's why 'the wise do not speak and those who speak are not wise'. How can the world know the real nature of Tao?

Duke Huan, seated high up in his hall, was reading out loud, and the wheelwright Pien was making a wheel in the courtyard below. Laying aside his hammer and chisel, Pien walked up the stairs, and interrupted the Duke.

'May I ask your Grace what words you are reading?'

The Duke said, 'The words of the sages.'

'Are those sages alive?' Pien asked.

'No, they're dead,' was the reply.

'Then,' said the wheelwright, 'what you, my ruler, are reading is only the dregs and sediments of dead men.'

The Duke, a lover of wisdom, became upset at this and said, 'How can you, a wheelwright, have anything to say about my book? If you can explain yourself, well and good. If you can't, you shall die!'

The wheelwright said, 'Your servant will look at the subject from the point of view of his own craft. In making a wheel, if I go at it gently, it's certainly pleasant enough, but the workmanship isn't very strong. If I have to push forcefully, that's an effort and the joints won't fit well. Neither too gentle nor too forceful: my hand knows how to do it in harmony with my heart, and a fine wheel is produced. But I can't tell you how to do it in words – there's a certain knack to it. I can't even teach this knack to my son, nor can my son learn it from me. That's why I'm seventy years old and am still making wheels.

'Now, these ancient sages of yours must have been just like me – they also had a certain knack that it wasn't possible for them to convey in words. If you'd been able to sit and learn from them, then perhaps you could've picked up that knack. But now they're dead and gone, and all you're reading is their dregs and sediments!'

CHAPTER TWO

Perfect Happiness

Perfect Happiness Is Doing Nothing

Under the sheltering blue sky can perfect happiness be found? Are there people who can keep their selves whole? If there are, what do they do? What do they practise? What do they avoid? What do they concern themselves with? Where do they go? Where do they avoid? What gives them pleasure? What do they dislike?

What the world values is money, status, long life and fame. What it delights in is good times, leisure, rich delicacies, fine clothes, beautiful colours and pleasant music.

What it despises is poverty and a wretched life-style, a short life, weakness and notoriety. What people consider bitter is when their bodies aren't able to find rest and ease, when their mouths don't taste rich food, when they're not elegantly clothed, when their eyes don't see beautiful sights, and their ears never hear sweet music.

If they can't get these things they become unhappy, and are obsessed with fears. Their thoughts are all about the body – aren't they foolish?

Now the rich embitter their lives by incessant work, accumulating more wealth than they can use. When they act like this for their bodies, they treat it as something external to themselves, lacking contentment with what they have. Those who seek power and fame carry on this pursuit day and night, worried only about how skilful their methods are. When they act like this they treat their body carelessly, constantly surrounded by anxiety.

The birth of a person is also the birth of their sorrow. Someone who lives a long life becomes more and more senile and the longer he lasts the longer his anxiety not to die. How great is this bitterness! When a person acts like this for his body, it's for a very distant result.

As to what ordinary people do, and where they find happiness, I can't tell whether this happiness is real or not. I see them in pursuit of it, rushing with grim determination, as if they're unable to stop. But what they call happiness wouldn't be that to me, and yet I can't say there's no happiness in it. Is there really such happiness, or isn't there?

I consider 'doing nothing' to be the greatest happiness, while ordinarily people consider 'doing nothing' to be a great evil. Hence it is paradoxically said, 'Perfect happiness is to be without happiness; the highest praise is to be without praise.'

The right or wrong of this point of happiness can't be determined according to the view of the world. Nevertheless, 'doing nothing' or 'not trying' to obtain happiness can actually judge both the right and the wrong. Since we consider perfect happiness to be in keeping oneself alive, it's only by 'doing nothing' that this can be achieved.

I'll try to explain this a bit more:

Heaven does nothing, and so maintains its serenity.
Earth does nothing, and so has its peace.
By the union of these two non-active forces, everything is
    produced.
How vast and imperceptible is this process!
Things seem to come from nowhere!
How imperceptible and vast!
We can't begin to see it!

All things in all their variety grow from this inaction. Hence the saying, 'Heaven and Earth do nothing, and yet there is nothing that remains undone.'

But can we find anyone who trusts the universe enough to live according to 'doing nothing'?

The Eight Delights

Humanity has eight treasures:

> *pleasure in seeing leads to excessive pursuit of brilliant colours*
> *pleasure in hearing to excessive pursuit of attractive sound*
> *pleasure in goodness disturbs natural virtue*
> *pleasure in justice is in opposition to reason*
> *pleasure in rituals helps aesthetic creation*
> *pleasure in music leads to sensuous melodies*
> *pleasure in wisdom helps create ingenious devices*
> *pleasure in knowledge contributes to fault-finding*

If we could all discover how to stay rooted in our natural instincts, then whether we retain or lose these eight treasures would make no difference whatsoever. But if we can't discover how to stabilise ourselves internally, then these eight treasures become unevenly developed or else violently suppressed, and our world is thrown into confusion.

When people begin to magnify these eight treasures and even yearn for them, then how great is the deception practised on the world! Therefore the superior person, who does not feel a need to take part in worldly affairs, will find it best to 'do nothing'. In the policy of action-less action, the superior person can rest in the natural instincts which he has been given. That's why the person who can administer a state, respecting it as he respects his own body, may have the state committed to him, and the person who can administer the state by loving it as he loves his own body, may have it entrusted to him.

Therefore, if the superior person maintains and preserves the vital chi lodged in his body, and doesn't show off his powers of seeing and hearing, then when, in meditation, he stays motionless as a corpse, his dragon-like presence will still be seen. Even when the superior person is profoundly silent, the thunder of his words still resounds. When his actions are unseen like those of a spirit, all heavenly influences will follow them. When he is completely unconcerned and does nothing, his sympathetic vibrations will attract and gather all things round him.

Why does he need to do anything more for the good conduct of the world?

Achieving Our Purpose

A sense of complete pleasure is what is meant by 'achieving our purpose'.

What the ancients called 'achieving our purpose' didn't mean acquiring official carriages and crowns. It simply meant that nothing more was needed than this achievement for their pleasure. Today what is called 'achieving our purpose' means getting more and bigger carriages and crowns. But crowns and carriages belong to the body and don't touch our innate nature.

When worldly goods come our way, it's only temporarily. Only happening for a time, you can't stop their coming or their going. Therefore we shouldn't for the sake of worldly goods pursue our purpose, nor because of distress and difficulties resort to conventional thinking. Neither seeking goods nor pursuing conventional thinking will lead to the happiness we need, which is simply to be free from anxiety. If we lose happiness when we lose what is transient, this shows that the pleasure it provided was worthless.

Hence it is said, 'Those who lose themselves in the desire for things, and lose their innate nature by studying what is conventional, must be considered people who turn things upside down.'

The Mind of a Real Person

Don't pursue fame: do only the inevitable.
Don't make plans: bank on Tao.
Don't make yourself busy: respond to events.
Know only that you don't know.

Wander freely in the infinite, but leave no trace behind.
Fulfil the potential Heaven has given you, but act as if you
received nothing.
Just be empty.

The Real Person of the Tao uses his mind like a mirror. It grasps nothing and anticipates nothing. It reflects what is before it, but doesn't retain it.

Thus the Real Person deals successfully with all things, without effort.

The Joy of Heaven

Some people by their stillness become sages, and by their actions – kings. Doing nothing, not striving, they're honoured. In their plain simplicity, no one in the world can compete with them for excellence.

Clear understanding of the power of Heaven and Earth is called 'The Great Root' and 'The Great Origin'. Those who have it are in harmony with Heaven, and through it are able to equalise all differences in the world, maintaining themselves in harmony with humanity. Being in harmony with humanity is called the Joy of Humanity, while being in harmony with Heaven is called the Joy of Heaven.

Chuang Tzu said,

> *'My teacher! My teacher!*
> *He grinds and mixes all life, but doesn't consider himself cruel.*
> *He benefits all ages, but doesn't think he's benevolent.*
> *He's older than the highest antiquity, but doesn't think he's old.*
> *He covers Heaven and sustains Earth, shaping and creating all forms, yet he doesn't think he's skilful.'*

This is called the Joy of Heaven.

The teaching says, 'Those who know the Joy of Heaven during their life act like Heaven, and at death undergo transformation like other things. In their stillness they're like Yin, and their movements flow like Yang.'

Therefore, the one who knows the Joy of Heaven makes no complaint against Heaven, finds no fault with humanity, isn't reliant on material objects, and suffers no hostility from spirits.

The teaching says, 'His movements are those of Heaven and his stillness is that of Earth. His heart is one, and he rules over the world. The spirits of his dead ancestors don't worry him, and his soul isn't troubled. His words, proceeding from emptiness and stillness, reach to Heaven and Earth, and communicate with all living things.'

This is called the Joy of Heaven, and it forms the mind of the sage, allowing him to nurture everything under the sky.'

Rejecting Power

Emperor Yao wanted to resign the throne to the hermit Hsu Yu and told him, 'When the sun and moon are both shining, isn't it difficult for a torch to give off light? When it's raining, isn't it a waste to continue watering the fields?

'If you, great master, take over as sovereign, the kingdom will immediately be well governed. If I continue to rule, I'll only be aware of my inadequacies. I beg to resign the throne to you.'

Hsu Yu replied, 'You, Sir, already govern the kingdom and it's well run. If in these circumstances I take your place, wouldn't people say I'm doing it solely for reputation? But reputation is only a shadow of reality. Shall I merely be playing the role of a shadow?

'The sparrow makes its nest in the deep forest, but only needs a single twig. The tapir drinks from the river, but only takes enough to fill its belly.

'Though the chef isn't attending to the oven, the waiters and guests wouldn't leave their wine and rush to start cooking.

'Return home, Sir. I will have nothing to do with the throne.'

What Is Distress?

Yuan Hsien, a former student of Confucius, was living in Lu. His tiny house, whose walls were only a few paces wide, looked as if it was thatched with a crop of new-mown grass. The brushwood door was broken, with branches of a mulberry tree for side-posts. The windows were formed by earthenware jars stuck in the wall, stuffed with some coarse rags. The roof leaked, and the ground was damp. Nevertheless, there he sat contentedly, strumming his lute and singing.

Tzu Kung, another of Confucius' students, wearing an inner robe of purple silk enfolded within an outer one of dazzling white, and riding in a carriage drawn by two large horses, went to visit him.

Yuan Hsien met him at the gate wearing a cap made of bark, slippers without heels, and with a stalk of hellebore for a staff.

'I'm sorry,' said Tzu Kung, 'to see you in such distress.'

Yuan Hsien answered, 'I've heard that to have no money is to be poor, and to be unable to carry one's learning into practice is to be distressed. I am indeed poor, but not in distress.'

Tzu Kung shrank back in embarrassment.

Yuan Hsien laughed and said, 'To act with the desire of being praised, to pretend to be non-partisan yet be biased, to learn in order to impress, to teach for the sake of profit, to conceal one's real intentions under the cloak of goodness and justice, and to flaunt one's carriages and horses – these are things I just can't bear to do.'

Advice from a Border Guard

Emperor Yao was touring in Hua, when the border guard noticed him and decided to offer blessings. He shouted out, 'May you live long!' This disturbed Yao, who told him to be quiet. But the guard went on, 'May the sage become rich!' Yao again tried to quiet him, but the guard continued, 'May the sage have many children!'

After Yao tried again to shut him up, the guard said, 'Long life, riches, and many children are what most people wish for. Why don't you want them?'

Yao replied, 'Many children bring many fears, riches bring only troubles and long life gives rise to endless problems.

These three things don't help to nourish virtue and therefore I resist them.'

The guard replied, 'At first, I considered you to be a sage but now I see you're just a nobleman. Heaven, in giving birth to multitudes of people, is sure to have arranged something for them to do. If you had many children they would each have a chance to do something, so what would you have to fear? If you were rich, and shared it with others, what troubles would you have?

> *'The sage dwells like a quail*
> *and is fed like a fledgling.*
> *He moves like a bird through the air*
> *and leaves no trace of his flight.*
> *When the whole world has Tao*
> *he shares in the general prosperity.*
> *When Tao is lost, and disorder prevails,*
> *he cultivates his virtue by himself.*
> *After a thousand years, weary of the world,*
> *he leaves it, and ascends among the immortals.*
> *He mounts on the white clouds,*
> *and arrives at the place of the Supreme One.*

'The three troubles you mention don't touch him, and he's always free from misfortune. So what disgrace would there be?'

The border guard shook his head in disgust and left Yao behind. But now Yao scampered after him, saying, 'I beg to ask about...' But the other man, with a gesture of dismissal, said, 'Get lost!'

Without Desires

Hui Tzu asked Chuang Tzu, 'Can a human being really live without feelings?'

Chuang Tzu said, 'He can.'

Hui Tzu said, 'But how can you call him human if he's without feelings?'

Chuang Tzu said, 'Tao gives him his appearance and Heaven gives him a body. Why shouldn't we call him human?'

Hui Tzu argued, 'Since you call him human, can he really be without feelings?'

Chuang Tzu replied, 'You misunderstand what I mean by feelings. What I mean is, he doesn't harm his body by indulging his tastes and passions. He accepts life as it comes, and allows it to continue in its own way.'

Hui Tzu replied, 'If he doesn't interfere with life, how does he survive?'

Chuang Tzu said, 'The Tao gives him his appearance. Heaven gives him a body. And he doesn't, by his personal tastes and passions, do any harm to his body. That's all!

'But you, Sir, tire your spirit on external things, and exhaust all your vital chi. You lean against a tree, philosophising, or fall asleep grasping your lute. Heaven gave you a human form, yet you wear it out with endless discussions.'

Swimming Free

Chuang Tzu and Hui Tzu were walking on the bridge over the River Hao, when Chuang Tzu said, 'Look how the fish come to the surface and swim around so freely – that's what fish really enjoy!'

Hui Tzu said, 'You're not a fish. How do you know what makes a fish happy?'

Chuang Tzu responded, 'You're not me. So how do you know that I don't know what fish enjoy?'

Hui Tzu said, 'I'm certainly not you, and so I don't know what you know, but you're definitely not a fish, and that proves that you don't know what makes fish happy.'

Chuang Tzu replied, 'Let's return to your original question. You said to me, "*How* do you know what makes a fish happy?" You already knew that I knew it, when you put the question to me. And I know it because of how you and I enjoy ourselves strolling freely together on this bridge.'

The Time Is Not Right

Chuang Tzu, wearing a patched cloak of coarse cloth, with his shoes tied together with string, was passing by the King of Wei, who said to him, 'How great, Master, is your distress!'

Chuang Tzu replied, 'It's poverty, not distress! If a scholar follows the Tao and its power, but can't put it into practice, then he's said to be in distress. Tattered clothes and worn out shoes are signs of poverty, but not of distress. This is what we call "not meeting with the right time".

'Hasn't Your Majesty ever seen monkeys climbing? When they're among plane trees and oaks, they grasp and twist the branches with their hands and feet, and nimbly use their tails to wrap themselves with leaves, so not even the greatest archers can shoot them.

'When, however, they're among prickly mulberry or date trees, and other thornbushes, they move cautiously, glancing sideways, and tremble with fear. It's not that their sinews and bones have lost suppleness, but the environment is unsuitable for them, and they can't show off their agility.

'Now, if my environment has a benighted ruler and

corrupt ministers, even if I wanted not to, how could I possibly avoid distress?'

The Success of the Superior Man

Confucius was stranded between Chen and Tsai, and for seven days had eaten no cooked food, only a vegetable broth without rice. He looked completely exhausted, yet he sat contentedly playing his lute and singing inside his room.

Yen Hui was outside picking vegetables, while Tzu Lu and Tzu Kung were talking. They said to Yen Hui, 'The Master was twice driven from Lu, he had to flee from Wei, the tree he rested under in Sung was cut down, and he was in extreme poverty in Shang. Now he is held here in a state of siege and anyone could take him prisoner or kill him without blame. And yet here he sits, playing and singing his lute without a break. Can a superior man be so lacking in shame?'

Yen Hui didn't know what to say, so he reported the conversation to Confucius. Confucius put his lute down and said, 'Lu and Tzu are petty men. Bring them in, and I'll explain it to them.'

When they came in, Tzu Lu said, 'I would describe your present situation as one of extreme distress.'

Confucius replied, 'What kind of talk is this! When the superior man flows with Tao, that is his success. When such freedom is denied him, that's his failure. Now I hold fast to the Tao of goodness and justice, and with them confront the troubles of a disordered age. How can you describe me as being in extreme distress?

'Therefore, looking inside and examining myself, I have no problems with my Tao. Though I may encounter great difficulties, I don't lose my virtue. It's when winter's cold has come, and the frost and snow are on the ground, that we know the true inner power of the pine and cypress trees. This difficult siege is actually a blessing for me.'

Confucius then calmly picked up his lute and began to play and sing. But now Tzu Lu hurriedly grabbed a shield and began to dance, while Tzu Kung said in admiration, 'Before, I didn't know the majestic height of Heaven nor the profound depth of the Earth.'

The ancients who found Tao were happy both in extremity and when flowing in freedom. Their happiness was independent of both these conditions. The Tao and the Te! Let the people have these and distress and success will come to them like wind and rain, like the natural cycles of cold and heat.

Rejecting Power Two

Chuang Tzu was fishing in the River Pu when the King of Chu sent two officers to convey this message: 'I wish to trouble you with the administration of all my lands.'

Chuang Tzu kept holding his rod and without looking round said, 'I understand that in Chu there's a sacred tortoise shell, 3,000 years old, which the King keeps in his ancestral temple, covered with a rich cloth. Do you think it was better for the tortoise to die, and leave its shell to be honoured in this way, or would it have been better to be alive, dragging its tail through the mud?'

One of the officers said, 'It would be better for it to live.'

Chuang Tzu nodded and said, 'Then go away. I'll keep on dragging my tail after me through the mud.'

CHAPTER THREE

In the Beginning

The Great Origin

At the very origin of all things nothing existed.
Since there was nothing, nothing could be named.
In this state of emptiness the One arose:
the very first existence, but without form or shape.
From this One all things could be produced,
receiving their Te or essential character.

The formless One divided into the Yin and Yang,
and Heaven and Earth were made.
Yin and Yang continues endlessly in operation,
and all things are produced.

As things are completed, they have their distinct forms,
which we call shapes.
Shape is the body preserving within it the spirit,
and each shape and spirit has its own innate Nature.

When our Nature has been properly cultivated,
it returns to its original and essential character.
When the original essence is recaptured,
there exists the same condition as at the very origin.

Being the same, it is empty,
being empty, it is great.
It is like the closing of a bird's beak
which silences its singing.

That closing and silencing is like the union
of Heaven and Earth at the very beginning.
This union may appear dull and stupid,
but it contains the mysterious,
the same mystery
that existed at the very origin.

It's the same as the Great Submission to the Natural Course
of things.

Losing the Original Condition

The people of old, when life was still chaotic, shared a simple
tranquillity with the whole world. In those times Yin and
Yang were in harmony, and their movement and rest proceeded without any disturbance. The four seasons followed
their regular times. Not a single thing received any injury,
and no living creature came to an early death.

Although people had knowledge, they had no occasion to
use it. This is what is called the state of Perfect and Primal
Unity. In those times no one took deliberate action, but only
practised constant spontaneity.

In this age of perfect virtue the wise weren't valued, and
the able weren't employed. The rulers were thought of as
just the higher branches of a tree and the people like deer in
the forest. They were upright and correct, without knowing
that to be so is justice. They loved one another, without
knowing that to do so was goodness. They were honest and
dependable, without knowing that this was loyalty. They
were trustworthy, without knowing that this was good faith.
In their spontaneous actions they assisted each other, without thinking that they were being generous. Therefore their
actions left no trace, and there was no record of their affairs.

The people have a regular and constant nature. They
weave cloth to wear and plough the ground to get food. This

is their common Virtue. They are all one in this, and don't form themselves into separate cliques. They would still be constituted like this if left to their natural tendencies. Therefore in the age of perfect virtue people walked along slowly and confidently, and looked steadily forward.

At those times, there were no footpaths or tunnels through the mountains, and on the lakes there were no boats or bridges. All creatures lived in groups and their settlements were close to each other. Birds and beasts multiplied into flocks and herds while the grass and trees grew luxuriant and tall. In this condition the birds and beasts could be led without ropes and the nests of the magpie could be approached and peeped into.

In the age of perfect virtue, men lived in common with birds and beasts, and were on terms of equality with all creatures, forming one family. How could they know about the distinctions of rulers and peasantry? Equally without knowledge, they didn't leave the path of their natural virtue. Equally free from desires, they were in a state of pure simplicity. In that state of pure simplicity, the people could follow their true nature.

This condition of excellence deteriorated and decayed, till Sui Jen and Fu Hsi arose and commenced their administration, and when the world complied with their methods the state of unity was lost.

Deterioration and decay continued until the Emperors Yao and Shun began to administer the world. These two introduced the method of governing by decrees and grand plans, thus corrupting the purity of nature and destroying simplicity.

They abandoned Tao, substituting goodness for it, and pursued the course of random and haphazard virtue. After this, they left their innate nature and followed the impulses of their minds. One clever mind after another merged their knowledge, but were unable to provide peace for the world.

Then they added ritual and ceremony, and went on to make these more and more numerous. These elaborate forms extinguished primal simplicity, till the heart was swamped by them.

After this the people were confused and disordered, and had lost the way that allowed them to return to their true nature, and bring back their original condition.

Preserving Tao

It's easy to see how the world abandoned Tao, and so Tao in its turn abandoned the world. The world and Tao having separated, how can the people who follow Tao make an impact on the world? And how can the world rise again to an appreciation of Tao?

Since Tao had no means of making an impact on the world, and the world had no means of rising to an appreciation of it, though sages might appear in towns and cities, their power was hidden. Hidden, but not because they themselves sought to hide it.

Those whom the ancients called 'Hidden Scholars' didn't conceal themselves or refuse to be seen. They didn't hold back their words, and refuse to speak. They didn't hide their wisdom, and refuse to share it. But the times they lived in were badly disordered. If the times had allowed them to act widely in the world, they would have returned everything to a state of Oneness, without anyone knowing how they did it. When disordered times blocked them from such action, they sunk their roots deeper in themselves, remained in utter tranquillity, and waited. By doing this they preserved Tao in themselves, never losing it.

The ancients who preserved Tao in themselves didn't try by sophisticated reasoning to explain their knowledge. They didn't seek to understand everything in the world, nor to comprise all the virtues in it. Solitary and cautious, they remained exactly where they were, and sought only the restoration of their own nature. Why did they need to bother with any other action?

Tao is not something that can be pursued, nor all of its characteristics known down to the smallest detail. Little knowledge is injurious to those characteristics and meddling actions are harmful to Tao. Hence it was said, 'They simply rectified themselves.'

Voluntary Retirement

When Yao was ruling the country, he appointed Po Cheng Tzu Kao as a governor of one of the states. After Yao the throne passed to Shun, and from Shun to Yu. At this point Po resigned his commission and returned home.

Yu, upset at Po's departure, went to see him, and found him ploughing his fields. Yu hurried to him, bowed low, stood up, and said, 'When Yao ruled, you, Sir, were appointed governor. Yao gave his sovereignty to Shun, and Shun gave his to me, at which point you, Sir, resigned your commission, and I now find you farming here. Can I ask the reason why?'

Tzu Kao stopped ploughing and said, 'When Yao ruled the country, the people did what was right without being offered rewards, and they were in awe of doing wrong without the threat of punishment. Now you employ both rewards and punishments, and still the people aren't good. Consequently, their virtue will from this time decay and punishments will prevail. The disorder of future ages has its origin here. Why don't you just go away, Sir, and not interrupt my work?'

Saying this, he resumed ploughing and didn't look back.

CHAPTER FOUR

The Way of Heaven

天

The Mirror of the Mind

The Tao of Heaven flows ceaselessly,
bringing all forms to completion,
but leaves behind no trace of its presence.

This mysterious Tao the ancient emperors employed,
and everything under the sky bowed to them.
The sages follow this same Tao of Heaven,
and the whole world admires them.

To clearly understand the Tao of Heaven,
to be conversant with the Tao of the sages,
to comprehend the virtue of the emperors,
to discover the power running through the universe:
act completely spontaneously,
appear to know nothing,
but remain centred in stillness.

The sage isn't still because he thinks it's good to be still. It's
because nothing disturbs his mind that he's able to be still.
    When water is still, its smooth surface reflects in detail
your mouth and eyebrows. It's a perfect level, and the greatest carpenter learns from it. If this is the clearness of still
water, how much greater is that of the human spirit! The still

mind of the sage is the mirror of Heaven and Earth, the reflection of all life.

Emptiness, stillness, calm, simplicity, quiet, silence and doing nothing – these share the pattern and order of Heaven and Earth, and are the natural characteristics of the mind of Tao.

Therefore the emperors, kings and sages discovered in this their place of peace. Resting, they became empty. From their emptiness arose fullness, and from their fullness came subtle awareness of life.

From their emptiness came stillness. Stillness was followed by movement, and their movements were successful.

From stillness came 'doing nothing'. Doing nothing, not striving, they entrusted responsibilities to others. Doing nothing, not striving, they were content and happy. When you achieve that feeling of happiness, anxieties and worries find no resting place, and the years of life are many.

Emptiness, stillness, calm, simplicity, quiet, silence, and doing nothing are the root of all things. When this is understood, we find a superior ruler on the throne, aided by excellent ministers. When these qualities are used in a high position, we find the virtues of emperors and kings – the sons of Heaven. When they are used in a low position, we find the Tao of the mysterious sages – the Way of the uncrowned kings.

Using these qualities to withdraw and enjoy themselves at leisure by rivers and seas, among the hills and forests, we find the scholars who are submissive to this Tao. When they use it to volunteer for active life to comfort their age, their merit and fame is great, and all the world becomes united as one.

The Mind of Heaven

Prime Minister Shun asked Emperor Yao, 'How does Your Majesty use his mind?'

The Emperor replied, 'I'm not arrogant towards the help-less and don't neglect the poor. I mourn for those who die, care for their infant children, and extend compassion to their widows. This is how I use my mind.'

Shun replied, 'That's fine, as far as it goes, but it's not what is called Great.'

'Then what do you think I should do?' asked the Emperor.

Shun replied, 'When a ruler possesses the virtue of Heaven, in order to foster action, he must remain in stillness. Heaven is high and the Earth is calm. The sun and moon simply shine, and the four seasons follow one another. Day and night have their regular pattern, and bring on the clouds which cause rain to disperse.'

Yao said, 'So I've just been making trouble for myself! You want me to be in harmony with Heaven, while I've tried to be in harmony with humanity.'

The ancients thought Heaven and Earth were great, and the Yellow Emperor, Yao and Shun united in admiring them. Therefore the kings of old did nothing, but merely tried to imitate the Tao of Heaven and Earth.

Six Types Of People

To have a rigid and arrogant mind;
to disdain the world, and pursue their own ways;
to be full of lofty principles;
to insolently slander others;

This is favoured by scholars who live in isolation, who always blame the world, and who stand apart with a weary look.

To preach about goodness, justice, loyalty, and faithfulness;
to be humble and frugal, selfless and courteous;

This is indicative of self-cultivation and is practised by scholars who want to reform the world – teachers and preachers – and who pursue their studies at home and abroad.

To brag about their merit;
to build a great reputation;
to insist on the protocol between ruler and ministers;
to sort out distinctions between high and low;
their one object the promotion of power.

This is favoured by courtiers, people who honour their ruler and strengthen the state, and whose one desire is to seize other states.

To retreat to marshes and lakes;
to live in solitary places;
to occupy themselves with fishing and boating;
to live in ease;
to do nothing.

This is the life of scholars of the rivers and seas, people who avoid society and desire to live in idleness.

To huff and to puff;
to inhale and exhale the breath;
to expel their old breath and take in the new;
to stretch and twist their necks and bodies;
all this simply shows a desire for longevity.

This is the Tao of the scholars who manipulate their chi, who nourish their breath and body, and wish to live as long as possible.

As to those who maintain good character without a rigid
   mind;
who practise self-cultivation without goodness and justice;
who govern successfully without merit or fame;
who find peace without resorting to rivers and seas;
who live long without managing their breath;
who can forget everything and still possess all things;
whose calm serenity is unlimited, while all good things
   accompany them.

People like this are Real People who pursue the Way of
Heaven and Earth, and display the integrity of sages.

That's why it is said, 'Serenity, detachment, silence, quiet,
emptiness, and doing nothing: these are the root of Heaven
and earth and are the substance of Tao and its power.'

Qualities of the Sage

The ancient teaching says, 'The sage is entirely peaceful, so
his mind is evenly balanced and at ease. This even balance
and ease appears in his serenity and detachment. In this
state of balance and ease, of serenity and detachment,
anxieties and anguish don't affect him, and no harmful
influences assault him. His Te, or power, is complete, and his
spirit continues undiminished.

'The life of the sage can be compared to the action of
Heaven and his death is the transformation common to all
things. In his stillness his power is the same as the Yin, and
in movement his actions are like the Yang. He takes no
initiative in producing either happiness or calamity.

'The sage responds to the influences acting on him, and
moves only when he feels the pressure. He acts only when he
has no other choice. He discards knowledge and memories,
and merely follows the pattern of his Heaven-given nature.

Therefore he suffers no calamity from Heaven, no attachment to things, no blame from people, and no disapproval from the spirits of the dead.

> 'The sage's life seems to just drift along;
> his death seems to be a resting;
> he doesn't have anxious thoughts;
> he doesn't make plans;
> his enlightenment is hidden;
> his good faith isn't contrived;
> he sleeps untroubled by dreams;
> he wakes untroubled by cares;
> his spirit is simple and pure;
> his soul is never weary.

'Empty and selfless, calm and detached, the sage is in harmony with the virtue of Heaven.'

Therefore the teaching says, 'Sorrow and joy are distortions of virtue; goodness and evil are transgressions of virtue; likes and dislikes show a failure of the mind. So for the mind to be free from sorrow and joy is to have perfected virtue. For the mind to be unified and unchanging is the perfection of stillness. To be conscious of no opposition is the perfection of emptiness. To have no attachment to external things is the perfection of indifference. And to have no feelings of dissatisfaction is the perfection of purity.'

The Righteous Butcher

When King Chao of Chu lost his kingdom, the sheep-butcher Yueh followed him into exile. When the King recovered his throne, he decided to reward those who had been loyal. When it was his turn, Yueh said, 'When our Great King lost his kingdom, I lost my business. When His Majesty got back his kingdom, I in turn got back my business. My position and income have been recovered – why does he need to reward me?'

The King, on hearing this, said, 'Force him to take the reward!'

But Yueh said, 'It wasn't through any fault of mine that the King lost his kingdom, so I didn't deserve any punishment. And since it wasn't through any achievement of mine that he recovered his kingdom, I don't expect to be rewarded.'

The King said, 'I want to meet this man.'

But Yueh said, 'According to the law, great reward should be given for great achievement, and only then should the recipient be introduced to the King. Now I didn't have sufficient knowledge to preserve the kingdom, and my courage was insufficient to die for it. When the armies of Wu entered, I was afraid, and fled for my life. It wasn't out of loyalty that I followed the King. Now he wishes, disregarding the law, and in violation of our conventions, to admit me to his presence. I wouldn't like the people to hear this spoken about me throughout the kingdom.'

The King said to Tzu Chi, the Minister of War, 'The sheep-butcher's position is low, but his declaration of what is right is very high. Will you ask him to accept the position of one of my three most distinguished ministers?'

Yueh replied to this honour, 'I know that the position of a distinguished minister is nobler than a sheep-butcher's stall, and the salary of 10,000 chung is more than a sheep-butcher's profits. But how can I, through desire of rank and income, give my ruler the name of an irresponsible benefactor of his gifts? I dare not accept, but would prefer to return to my stall.'

The Voice

Tseng Tzu lived in Wei. He wore an old robe quilted with hemp, whose outer layer was missing. His face looked worn and emaciated and his hands and feet were hard and callused. He often lived for three days without lighting a fire and ten years between new clothes. If he tried to put his cap on straight, the straps would break; if he tightened the lapels of his robe, his elbows would poke through; when he put on his shoes, the heels would separate at the back.

Yet, dragging his shoes along, he sang the Hymns of Shang with a voice that filled Heaven and Earth as if it came from a bronze bell or a stone chime. The King couldn't convince him to be a minister and no feudal prince could make him their friend.

So it is that one who nourishes the soul forgets the body, one who nourishes the physical form forgets all thoughts of gain, and one who carries out the Tao forgets all about the mind.

The Nine Tests

Confucius said, 'It's more difficult to approach people's minds than a position defended by mountains and rivers, and more difficult to know than Heaven itself.

'Heaven shows its seasons of spring and autumn, of winter and summer, and its times of morning and evening. But humanity has an impenetrable appearance, and true feelings lie deeply hidden.

'Thus some people have faces that look honest, yet they can be excessively mean. Others are truly gifted, but they look as if they have no ability. Some appear as airheads, yet they have far-reaching plans. Others look solid, but can be turned around. Others look slow, yet they can hustle.

'This is why those who hurry to do what's right as if it would quench their thirst will soon scamper from it as if it were a fire.

'So the superior man observes those working for him at a distance to test their loyalty, and observes them nearby to test their respect. By giving them difficult tasks, he tests their ability. By questioning them suddenly, he tests their knowledge. By giving them a deadline, he tests their good faith. By entrusting them with wealth, he tests their goodness. By informing them of imminent danger, he tests their resolve. By getting them drunk, he tests their temperament. By placing them with all kinds of people, he tests their sexuality.

'By these nine tests of their qualities people can be discovered.'

Instructions from a Boy

The Yellow Emperor, Huang Ti, went to see Tai Kwei at Chu Tzu Mountain. When his group arrived at the wilds of Hsiang Cheng, the sages were all unsure about their location, and couldn't find anyone to ask the way.

Just then they saw a boy pasturing horses, and asked him, 'Do you know the way to Chu Tzu mountain?' He said he did, and he also knew where Tai Kwei was living.

'This is a strange boy,' said Huang Ti. 'How did he know we wanted to visit Tai Kwei? Let me ask him how to govern everything under Heaven.'

The boy said, 'Governing everything under Heaven is no different from what I am doing here – why should it be so difficult? When I was younger, I enjoyed myself by roaming within the six confines of space, but then my eyesight began to suffer. A wise elder told me, "Ride in the chariot of the sun, and roam in the wild of Hsiang Cheng." Now the problem with my eyes is a little better, and I am again enjoying myself roaming, but now outside the six confines of space.

'As to governing everything under Heaven, as I said it's just like this – no big problem!'

Huang Ti said, 'Ruling everything under Heaven is indeed not your problem, my son. Nevertheless, I would like to ask you about it.'

The little herder didn't want to answer, but Huang Ti insisted, so he said, 'How is looking after the world any different from taking care of horses? All you have to do is to remove anything that would injure the horses!'

The Yellow Emperor bowed twice to him, called him his Heavenly Master, and departed.

CHAPTER FIVE

The Wondrous One

Wonder

Does Heaven revolve?
Does the Earth stand still?
Do the sun and moon argue over their places?
Who directs all of these things?
Who holds it all together?
Who, by doing nothing, creates all of this?

Is there some hidden spring
that forces them to turn?
Or is it that they just keep turning
and can't stop?

Do the clouds become rain?
Or does the rain form the clouds?
Who causes this abundance?
Who, by doing nothing, makes this incredible excess?

The winds rise in the north,
some blow west, others east,
while some rise upwards,
drifting who knows where.
Whose breath produces them?
Who, by doing nothing, creates all this activity?

I would really love to know their cause.

The Perfect Tao

Confucius, on a visit to Lao Tzu, asked him, 'Since we have some time together, can you tell me about the Perfect Tao?'

Lao Tzu replied, 'To find the most Perfect Tao, you must cleanse your mind with emptiness, wash your spirit white as snow, and strongly repress your knowledge.

'Tao is deep, and difficult to describe! I can only give you a sketch:

'The luminous is produced from the deepest dark;
the orderly is born from the formless;
the spiritual comes from Tao,
and the body from the quintessential.

'All things are produced from their bodily shapes:
Creatures with nine openings come from the womb,
and those with eight emerge from eggs.

'Tao's coming leaves no trace,
its going leaves no monument;
it enters by no door,
it dwells in no apartment:
but it extends in vast open space to all directions.

'Those who discover Tao are strong in body,
sincere and far reaching in thought,
sharp in hearing, clear in seeing.
Exercising their minds without fail
they respond accurately to everything.

'Without Tao, Heaven wouldn't be high,
Earth wouldn't be broad;
the sun and moon wouldn't revolve,
and nothing would prosper:
this is the operation of the Tao!

'The most extensive knowledge doesn't know it;
reasoning can't make people wise in it:
the sages rejected both these methods.

'However you try to add to it,
it can't be increased;
however you try to take from it,
it can't be diminished.

'This is what the ancient sages say about it:

'"How deep it is, like the sea!
How grand it is, like a mountain!
It begins again when it comes to an end,
carrying along and sustaining all life,
never fatigued or weary.

'"All things return to it,
and find their dependence on it:
this is the true character of Tao!"'

'Let's take as an example a woman born in China. She dwells here between Heaven and Earth, balanced between Yin and Yang, only temporarily as a woman, for one day she'll return to her source.

'Looking at her origin, when her life began, we have only a bit of goo in which her original breath is collecting. Whether her life will be long or her death early, what difference does it make? Life is just the name for a brief moment of time, insufficient to determine what is right and what is wrong.

'The fruits of trees and climbing plants have their distinctive patterns. Even human relationships, though troublesome, have an order and structure. The sage, when he encounters them, doesn't oppose them, and when he's negotiated his way through, doesn't seek to hold on to them.

He responds to everyone harmoniously according to his virtue. He greets them as a companion, according to his Tao. It was by following this path that the old emperors flourished, and the ancient kings arose.

'Our life is like a white colt
passing a narrow slit in a wall –
briefly glimpsed.
With a great push and surge all emerge;
gently and quietly all re-enter.

'By one transformation everything lives,
by another everything dies.
Living things are saddened by death;
but it's only the removal of a heavenly bow from its case,
the emptying of a heavenly satchel.
There may be confusion during the change,
as the spiritual and animal souls take their leave
and then the body follows:
this is the Great Returning home.

'That our body came from the formless,
and will return to it,
is what everyone knows,
but this doesn't disturb one who has Tao.

'This is something everyone talks about.
Those whose knowledge is complete don't need to discuss it;
such discussion shows their knowledge isn't complete.
Even the clearest minds do not meet Tao:
better to be silent than think too much about it.
The Tao can't be heard with the ears:
better to shut the ears than strain to hear it.

'This is what is called the Great Attainment.'

The Magnificent Ten

The Old Master said, It's Tao that supports and sustains all things. How magnificent is its immense influence! The superior person's mind should open to it.

Acting by doing nothing is Heavenly action.
Speech emerging naturally is a mark of true virtue.
Loving people and aiding things is goodness.
Uniting differences is being great.
Conduct free from ambition is being generous.
Living with a rich diversity is true wealth.
Clinging to your natural attributes is the guideline.
Perfecting those attributes is its foundation.
Conforming to Tao is being complete.
Protecting the will from pernicious influence is fulfilment.

When the superior person understands these ten things, she keeps all matters wrapped up in herself, showing the greatness of her mind. Through the outcome of her actions, all things stir and are attracted to her.

Such a person lets the gold stay hidden in the mountains,
and the pearls sleep in the deep waters.
She doesn't consider property or money to be a benefit
and avoids riches and honours.
She doesn't rejoice in long life,
nor grieve over early death.
She doesn't account prosperity a blessing,
nor is ashamed of poverty.

Given a choice, she would not grab the world's wealth as her private possession. Given a choice, she wouldn't want to rule the world as her private domain. Instead she clearly understands that all things belong to one treasury, and death and life form one continuous strand.

Before Heaven and Earth

Jan Chiu, one of Confucius' students, asked him, 'Can we know how it was before Heaven and Earth existed?'

Confucius replied, 'We can. It was the same then as now.'

Jan Chiu accepted the answer and left. But the next day, he said, 'Yesterday I asked whether we can know how it was before Heaven and Earth existed, and you, Master, said, "We can. As it is now, so it was of old." Yesterday I thought I understood you clearly, but today I am uncertain. Can you explain it to me?'

Confucius said, 'Yesterday you understood me clearly, because your spirit had understood my reply. Today you're uncertain, because you no longer trust your spirit, but are striving to think out the meaning.

'In what we are discussing, there is no past and no present, no beginning and no end. Could we say that there were grandchildren and children unless there had been earlier grandchildren and children?'

Jan Chiu was silent, so Confucius went on, 'Enough! Don't try to answer.

'We can't with life give birth to death; we can't with death bring death to life. Do death and life rely on each other? There is only the One which contains them both in its embrace.

'Is there something that existed before Heaven and Earth? Could that which existed first and which produced Heaven and Earth be a thing? That which creates things and gives each its distinct character can't itself be a thing. Things that are produced can't exist before there are other things to produce them, but there had to be that which made the first things. And this maker of the first things must still exist, the same now as before.

'The sages' love for others, which never ends, is based on this model.'

The Qualities of a King

The Old Master said,

> 'How still and deep lies Tao!
> How lucid in its clarity!
> Without it bronze and stone wouldn't resonate.
> Within they have the power of sound,
> but if they aren't struck, they remain silent.
> Who can discover the hidden qualities in all things?

'The person of kingly qualities remains detached, and is reluctant to get involved with the affairs of state. He roots himself in the source of his creativity, and watches his spirit grow. His inner qualities expand, and as he flows with the world, when things come his way, his mind accepts them and deals with them.

'If there were no Tao, his body would not have life, and his inner power, without the virtues of Tao, wouldn't be embodied. The person who preserves his body and lives the fullest life, who establishes the virtues of the Tao and clearly displays them, possesses the qualities of a king! Suddenly he surges forward, surprising everyone, and all things feel compelled to follow! This is what we call a leader.

> 'He sees in the deepest darkness.
> He hears where there is no sound.
> In the midst of the deepest darkness,
> he alone sees the glimmer.
> In the midst of a soundless abyss,
> he alone hears the harmony.
> Where depth sinks down to depth,
> he alone can perceive.
> Where mystery reveals deeper mystery,
> he alone discerns the subtle.

'In his dealings with others,
though he possesses only emptiness,
they get everything they seek.
He first surges ahead,
but later returns to his resting place.
Now great, now small;
now long, now short;
now distant, now near.'

The Great Pervader

This is the Great Tao.
   It has both reality and substance, but it does nothing and
has no material form.

A teacher can transmit it,
but can't guarantee its reception.
It can be found, but it can't be seen:
it is its own source, its own root.
Before there was Heaven and Earth,
from of old, there it was,
eternally existing.

From it came the mysterious existence of spirit,
from it came the mysterious existence of God.
It produced Heaven and Earth.
It is far above, yet can't be considered high.
It is below all space, yet can't be considered deep.
It was born before Heaven and Earth,
yet you can't say it has existed long.
It's older than the oldest antiquity,
yet you can't call it old.

No one knows its beginning,
no one knows its end.

You listen for it,
but can't hear its sound.
You look for it,
but can't perceive its shape.

It fills Heaven and Earth and envelops everything within the universe.

Holding Your Own

Shun asked his aide Chang, 'Can I get the Tao and hold it as my own?'

Chang said, 'Even your body isn't your own to hold – how can you expect to get and hold Tao?'

Shun continued, 'If my body isn't mine, then whose is it?'

Chang said, 'It's the shape given to you by Heaven and Earth. Life isn't yours to possess, it's the blended harmony of Yin and Yang, entrusted to you by Heaven and Earth. Your innate nature isn't yours to hold, it's bestowed on you by Heaven and Earth for you to act in accordance with it. Your children and grandchildren aren't yours to hold, they're like cast-off skins entrusted to you by Heaven and Earth.

'Therefore, when you walk, you don't know where you're going. When you stay somewhere, you have no idea where that really is. When you eat, you don't even know what you are tasting: all this is due to the strong Yang influence of Heaven and Earth.

'How then do you expect to get Tao and hold it as your own?'

The Political Theory of the Original Chi

The Great Primal Chi met the East Wind on the shore of the eastern sea, and the East Wind asked where it was going.

'I'm going', said Primal Chi, 'to the ocean.'

The East Wind asked, 'What for?'

Primal Chi said, 'The ocean has such a nature that the rivers which flow into it never fill it, and those which flow out of it never drain it. I intend to enjoy myself by rambling nearby.'

The East Wind replied, 'Aren't you concerned about people? Do you have anything to say about how sages rule?'

The Great Primal Chi said, 'Under the government of sages, all officials are appointed according to natural suitability. All promotions are made according to ability. Nothing is done until there is a complete survey of all the circumstances. Actions and words proceed from the sages' inner impulse, and the whole world is transformed.

'Wherever their hands point to and their looks direct, the people are sure to accomplish whatever they desire. This is what is called government by sages.'

'What about the virtuous?' continued the East Wind.

Primal Chi replied,

'The virtuous ones remain still,
and have no random thoughts.
When they act, it's without plan.
They don't store in memory
what's right or wrong,
what's good or bad.
They share what they have with everyone,
producing a state of satisfaction.
They dispense their gifts to everyone,
producing a state of peace.

'Timid, like motherless children;
Uncertain, like lost travellers.
Full of wealth and every necessity,
they don't know where it comes from.
Sufficient in food and drink,
they have no idea who gave it to them.

'That is how things are with the kindly and virtuous.'
    'What about people of the spirit?' continued the East Wind.

'Their spirits mount up on the light,
their bodies freed from limitations.
This we call being bright and ethereal.
They complete their destiny,
and leave no single potential unfulfilled.
They enjoy heaven and earth,
and life's conflicts dissolve.
All things return to their original nature,
merging with the mysterious darkness.'

CHAPTER SIX

Little and Large

Great Knowledge and Small Knowledge

In the Northern Ocean there's an enormous fish called Kun. It mutates into a bird called Peng whose back is vast like a mountain range. When this bird rouses itself and flies, its wings are like dark clouds eclipsing the sky.

In the ancient *Book of Wonders* we have these words: 'When the Peng takes off, its wings stir the waves for 1,000 miles. Then it rises high on a whirlwind for 30,000 miles, far above the misty clouds, and, bearing on its broad back the blue sky, it heads south for the Celestial Lake, and only rests after flying for six months.'

This is no different than the wind swirling the dust which quivers in the sunlight, and the breath of all living creatures as the wind blows them together. Is blue the real colour of the sky? Or is it just its distance and majesty that gives it this colour?

And what about the accumulation of water? If there is little, it won't have the strength to support a large boat. Pour a cup of water into a small hollow, and a seed will float on it like a little ship. Put the cup itself in, and it sinks to the earth. The water's shallow and the boat's large.

It's the same with the gathering wind. If it's not great, it will lack the strength to support large wings. The Peng ascends to the great height of 30,000 miles, and beneath him there's the huge mass of wind he depends on to support him. As he carries the blue sky on his back, and there's nothing to block his flight, he can head south.

A cicada and a little dove saw him flying by and laughed, saying, 'We try hard and fly towards an elm tree, and sometimes, before we even reach it, we lose strength and drop to the ground. What chance does this creature have of rising so high in the sky and heading south?'

A quail by a marsh laughed at him too and said, 'Where is he going? I spring up with a leap, slip down again after just a few metres, and then flap around in the bushes. This I consider the sheer perfection of flying. Who does he think he is?'

If you take a walk in the country and pack a lunch you return home with a full stomach. If you journey for 100 miles you must pack food for several days. And if you journey for 1,000 miles, you need to carry provisions for three months.

How can these tiny creatures know anything about this? Small knowledge is no match for great knowledge. Experience of a few years doesn't equal that of many.

How do we know this? The mushroom that appears in the morning and dies that same night hasn't a clue about the cycles of the moon. The chrysalis is ignorant about the cycles of spring and autumn. These are both short-lived.

This is the difference between the small and the great. This is why a person wise enough for one position, or whose conduct can establish peace in a village, or whose excellence can efficiently govern a small state, is sure to look on himself with the smug satisfaction of these small creatures.

But someone like Sung Yung Tzu, the Master of Simple Living, would have laughed at all of them. Though the whole world praised him, he wouldn't have done more, and if the whole world condemned him, he wouldn't alter his Tao. He knew the difference between his inner judgement and the judgement of others, so he distinctly marked out the boundary between glory and disgrace. And here, at this boundary, he stopped. Although people like Sung Yung Tzu are rare, there was still something he didn't establish.

Consider Lieh Tzu, who rode on the wind, drifting at ease, and returned after fifteen days. In the search for happiness he had no limitations. Although he could give up walking, there was still something even he had to depend on.

But suppose someone could rise on the natural energy of heaven and earth, ride on the six elemental breaths, and wander with pleasure in the infinite. What is he dependent on?

That's why it's said:

> 'The perfect person has no self,
> the spiritual person has no achievement,
> and the sage has no fame.'

The Great Victory

The worm is intrigued by the millipede, the millipede desires to be like the snake, and the snake envies the wind.

The worm said to the millipede, 'With my one leg I hop along and barely manage to get anywhere. But you have hundreds of feet to use. How do you manage?'

The millipede replied, 'It isn't so difficult. Haven't you ever seen someone spit? When he does, the largest gob is as big as a pearl, while the smaller drops fall like a great shower of mist. Mixed together, these drops are innumerable. I just put in motion the springs that have been set in me by Heaven, without knowing how I do it.'

The millipede in turn said to the snake, 'My legs carry me along, but I can't go as fast as you, who have no legs at all. Why is that?'

The snake replied, 'I move along by the inner design

given me by Heaven, and this can't be changed. What would I do with legs?'

The snake said to the wind, 'I move by twisting my backbone and ribs, and this is my body's mobility. But you rise with a blustering force in the North Sea, and go whirling to the South Sea – seemingly without a body. How is that?'

The wind said, 'It's true that I rise with a blustering force in the North Sea and go to the South Sea. But don't you think you're superior to me, since you can defeat me by raising your body against me, and trample me. Still, it is only I who can topple tall trees, and blow down great houses. Only I can do this.'

Therefore the One who overcomes all the small defeats can make a great victory. But only a sage can do this.

A Small Tragedy

Great knowledge is broad,
small knowledge is cramped.
Great speech is inspiring,
small speech is mere chatter.

When we sleep, our spirit communes outside;
when we awake, our body is free to wander.
Relationships lead to entanglement,
daily struggle of mind with mind.

Sometimes hesitant,
sometimes sly,
sometimes petty.

Small fears lead to anxiety,
great fears to terror.

When words fly off like arrows,
we have those who claim authority
to decide right and wrong.
Their speech composed like a covenant,
we have those who defend their opinions,
determined to gain victory.

But opinions, like the decay of autumn and winter,
are impermanent, and pass away day by day.
We are like a spray of water:
once released, we can't be re-gathered.
Stagnating like blocked drains,
our minds become old and dry, near death.
And when our minds draw near to death,
they can't be restored to youth.

Joy and anger;
sorrow and delight;
hope and fear;
uncertainty and strength;
wilfulness and lethargy;
enthusiasm and reticence.
All these moods,
like music from an empty reed,
or mushrooms rising from the damp earth,
endlessly succeed one another,
and who knows where they come from?

Let's stop!
Let them be!
Morning and night exist,
and through them we live.

If they didn't exist,
we wouldn't be here.

If we didn't exist,
then who would be aware?

This is close to the truth,
but I don't know why.
There should be a true ruler,
but I can't find a trace of its presence.
I am certain that it acts,
but I don't see its form.
I can feel it
but it has no form.

Your body has one hundred parts:
nine openings and six viscera,
all complete and correct.
Which part do you like best?
Do you like them all equally?
Or do you prefer the heart over the others?
Aren't they all your servants?
If they are servants,
how do they maintain order?
Does one rule over the others,
Or do they take it in turns
to be ruler and servant?
There must exist a True Ruler,
though you may not be able to find it.
And it doesn't really matter,
since its truth is evident.

Once you are born with a complete body,
your organism delivers until the end.
Whether clashing with others
or in harmony with them,
you run through life to the end,
like an unstoppable runaway horse.

Isn't it sad?
To sweat blood all your life
without seeing any result,
to become weary and worn out,
not knowing where to find rest.
Isn't this a pity?

We may say to give ourselves comfort
'At least I'm still alive!'
but what good is that?
When our body decays,
so does our mind –
it too must dissolve.
Wouldn't you agree that this is really tragic?
Is our life really so absurd?
Am I the only one who feels this?
Don't others see it too?

Dry Fish

When Chuang Tzu was young his family had nothing to eat. He went to borrow some rice from the Marquis of Chien Ho, who said, 'Of course! I will collect the tax revenue soon, and can then lend you three hundred ounces of silver. Will that do?'

Chuang Tzu flushed with anger and said, 'On the road yesterday, I heard someone calling out. Looking round, I saw a fish lying in the road, and I said, "Master fish, what are you doing here?" The fish said, "I am Minister of Waves in the Eastern Sea. Can you give me a gallon of water to keep me alive?"

'I replied, "Of course! I'm going south to see the Kings of Wu and Yueh, and I can then divert a stream from the Western River to flow here. Will that do?"

'The fish flushed with anger, and said, "I'm out of my own element, and can't do anything here for myself. If I could just get a gallon of water, I could keep myself alive. But if I follow your plan, you can look for me tomorrow in a dried-fish stall."'

Knowing Too Much

Knowledge was rambling north in the region of Dark Water. He ascended the heights of Imperceptible Slope, and bumped into Silent Do Nothing.

Knowledge said to him, 'I'm glad to have met you, because I have some questions to ask. What kind of thought and conscious reflection do we need to know the Tao? Where should we stay and what should we do to be secure in the Tao? Where is the starting point of the path that leads to the Tao?'

Silent Do Nothing just stared at him. Not only didn't he answer, but he didn't even know how to answer.

Knowledge, disappointed, returned south to the Bright Water, and ascended the height of the End of Doubt, where he found Reckless Blurter, of whom he asked the same questions.

Reckless Blurter replied, 'Ah, I know the answers, and I will tell ...' But just as he was about to speak, he forgot what he was going to say.

Knowledge, frustrated, returned to the Emperor's palace, where he saw The Yellow Emperor, Huang Ti, and put the questions to him. The Yellow Emperor said, 'Have no thought and no conceptions and you can come to know Tao. Stay in no particular place, do nothing and you can find a rest in Tao. Start anywhere, do not make plans and you will attain Tao.'

Knowledge replied, 'You and I know this, but those two didn't. Which of us is right?'

The Yellow Emperor replied, 'Silent Do Nothing is truly
right, Reckless Blurter has the appearance of being right,
and you and I are far from it.

'*Those who know do not speak,*
those who speak do not know.
The true sage teaches without words.

'*We can't force Tao to be ours:*
its power won't come when we call.
Though goodness can be practised,
justice may be attempted,
and rituals can be performed.
That's why it's said,
"When Tao was lost, its attributes appeared.
When its attributes were lost, goodness appeared.
When goodness was lost, justice appeared.
When justice was lost, rituals appeared."

'Now rituals are only the ornamental flowers of Tao, and the
beginning of disorder.

'Hence it's said, "The person who practises Tao daily does
less and less. Doing less and less she eventually arrives at
doing nothing. Having arrived at doing nothing, there is
nothing which she does not do."

'Take as an example an ordinary kitchen pan. If you
wanted to make it return to the original state of its materials,
wouldn't it be difficult to do so? It's only the Real Person who
can recapture the original state.

'*Life is the follower of death,*
and death is the forerunner of life.
Who knows their regulator?
Life begins with a coalescence of breath.
When it collects, there is life;
when it disperses, there is death.

'Since death and life depend on each other, why should I consider one of them bad? All things in life are one, but we consider life beautiful because of its spirit and wonder, and death ugly because of its stench and decay. But stench and decay transform into the spiritual and wonderful, and the spiritual and wonderful transform again into stench and decay.

'Hence it's said, "Under the sky there's only one breath of life, and the sages prize that unity."'

Knowledge said to The Yellow Emperor, 'I asked Silent Do Nothing and he kept quiet. Not only didn't he answer me, but he didn't even know how to answer. I asked Reckless Blurter, and though he wanted to tell me, he didn't, and even forgot my questions. Now I've asked you, and you know all about it. Why do you say that you're far from it?'

The Emperor said, 'Silent Do Nothing was truly right, because he didn't know anything. Reckless Blurter was nearly right, because he'd forgotten it. You and I are far from right, because we know far too much.'

Complete Knowledge

Our feet use only a small patch of earth, but walking into undiscovered territory we journey long distances. Our true knowledge is minute, but using it to journey into the unknown, we come to know what is meant by Heaven.

We know Heaven as the great unity, the great Yin, the great light, the great framer, the great unlimited, the great truth, and the great judge. This makes our knowledge complete.

As the great unity, we understand it;
as the great Yin, we unfold it;
as the great light, we contemplate it;
as the great framer, it creates everything;

as the great unlimited, everything embodies it;
as The great truth, we examine it;
as The great judge, we embrace it.

Heaven is everything to us, and to flow with it shows the highest intelligence. Hide in its impenetrable darkness, and contemplate its origin.

Doing this, your understanding will seem like stupidity, and your knowledge will seem like ignorance. Only by unknowing can we know Tao. When seeking, we must not set limits, yet we can't be limitless. Ascending and descending away from us, sometimes slipping from our grasp, Tao is always a reality, unchanged now as of old, and always full. Can't we call it the great display and expansion? Why shouldn't we ask about it? Why should we be so confused about it? If we begin with what doesn't confuse us, we can progress to what has confused us, until we can stop being confused. In this way we arrive at freedom from all confusion!

CHAPTER SEVEN

The Good, the Bad and the Ugly

Virtue

When a person has extraordinary inner qualities, then physical appearance will be ignored. But when people don't ignore what they should ignore, and *do* ignore what shouldn't be ignored, then it's a case of true oblivion.

The sage's mind finds its pleasure in wandering, and looks on knowledge as just shoots from an old tree stump, conventions as like glue, goodness as only a social grace, and great skills as tools for business.

The sage makes no plans – what need does he have for knowledge?

He doesn't divide the world – what does he need glue for?

He lacks nothing – what need does he have for goodness?

He has no career – what does he need to trade?

These four things nourish his Heavenly nature, and this nourishment is his Heavenly food. Since he's fed from Heaven, what need does he have for anything from people? He has a human form, but not human emotions. Since he has a human form, he associates with them. But without human emotions, right and wrong have no effect on him.

How insignificantly small is the body which connects him to humanity! How infinitely great is he in the unique perfection of his Heavenly Nature!

The Guru

Lieh Tzu went on a journey to Chi, but after travelling only half-way he came back. On his return he met the teacher Po Hun Wu Shan who wondered why he had come back so suddenly.

Lieh Tzu said, 'I was frightened.'

'What scared you?'

'On the way there I went into ten soup shops, and in five of them the soup was set down in front of me before anyone else.'

'But why should that frighten you?'

Lieh Tzu said, 'Although the inner quality of a person can be hidden, the body, like a traitor, lets it shine through. This display awes people, who then treat you as noble or a sage, and from this treatment problems arise.

'You see, soup-sellers sell food simply as a matter of business, and however much they sell, their profit is small, and their power nil. Yet if they treated me as someone special, how much more would a ruler of 10,000 chariots! His body worn out with the cares of his kingdom, his knowledge overwhelmed by his affairs, he would want to hand these affairs to me, and expect me to successfully conduct his government. This is what frightened me.'

Po Hun Wu Shan replied, 'Very perceptive! But if you persist in carrying yourself as you do, people will come to you for refuge.'

Not long after, Po Hun Wu Shan went to visit Lieh Tzu, and found the doorway full of visitors' shoes. He stood there, holding his staff upright, leaning his chin on it until his skin puckered. After standing like this for a while, he went away without saying a word.

The door-keeper went in and told Lieh Tzu who immediately grabbed his shoes and ran barefoot after the visitor.

When he overtook him at the outer gate, he said, 'Since

you've come for a visit, won't you give me some good advice?'

Po Hun Wu Shan replied, 'It's too late. I told you that people would flock to you, and so they have. It's not that you cause them to gather, they simply can't stop coming. What good did my warning do? What attracts them and makes them pleased is your extraordinary qualities. But you, in turn, will be influenced by this crowd, your inner nature will be disturbed, and nothing can be done about it.

'These people will not tell you this. The small words they speak are like poison to you. They don't perceive this, nor do they understand it. How will you separate yourself from them?

'The clever toil on, and the wise are sad. Those who are without skills search for nothing. They eat to the full, and wander idly around. They drift like a ship loosed from its moorings, and just aimlessly wander.'

Deformed Body, Intact Mind

There was once a hunchback named Shu. His body was so bent that his chin reached down to his belly and his shoulders were higher than the crown of his head. His five internal organs were crammed into his trunk, and his thighs pressed into his ribs.

By sewing and washing he was able to feed himself; by sifting and cleaning rice, he was able to support a family of ten. When the government wanted soldiers, Shu could hang around without fear. When there was difficult work to be done, he was passed over. When they gave grain to the sick, he always got three measures, as well as ten bundles of firewood.

If a man so deformed in body can still support himself and live out the years of his life, how much more could others accomplish, whose only deformity is in their minds!

The Reformed Sage

In the state of Lu, Confucius' home state, there was a man called Wang Tai, whose feet had long ago been amputated as punishment for some crime. Now he had set himself up as a teacher and had many students.

One of Confucius' students, Chang Chi, asked about him, 'Although Wang Tai is a cripple, he's followed by as many students as you, Master. He doesn't stand up and teach and he doesn't sit down and lecture. But even though his students arrive empty, they return home full. Is there really such a thing as teaching without words? While Wang's body is so imperfect, can his mind be complete? What sort of man is he?'

Confucius replied, 'This Master is a sage. In fact, I should go to him and become his student, and so should those who are not my equal! Why should only the state of Lu follow him? I will lead all under Heaven to do so.'

Chang Chi replied, 'He's a man who has lost his feet, yet you consider him your teacher – he must be very different from ordinary men. Is there a special way that he uses his mind?'

Confucius replied, 'Death and life are great considerations, but neither of them causes him to alter. Even if heaven and earth would overturn and fall, he would not blink an eyelid. He sees clearly into the primal truth, and while other things change, he doesn't. The transformations of things he considers their destiny, and he keeps true to their source, the Tao.'

Chang Chi said, 'What do you mean?'

'When we look at things,' said Confucius, 'and see that they're different, we discriminate between them, for example distinguishing the liver from the gall bladder, or the state of Lu from Wei. But if we could look at them without discrimination, and see the ways in which they're similar, we would see they are all in a unity.

'So it is with this teacher. He doesn't discriminate between the things his senses present to him, but instead his mind delights in the harmony of their excellent qualities. He looks only at the unity which belongs to them, and doesn't perceive their difference, or where they've suffered loss. So Wang looks on the loss of his feet as only the loss of so much earth.'

Chang Chi said, 'He seems to be entirely occupied with cultivating his innate self. By his knowledge he has discovered the nature of his mind, and uses his mind to attain the eternal mind. Why do people gather round him?'

Confucius replied, 'No one uses running water as a mirror, only still water will do – only the stillest water can still people, and keep them in contemplation of their real selves. To his students he is like that still water.

'Of those who receive life from the Earth, it's the pine and cypress trees which are best – they remain green both in winter and summer. Of those given life from Heaven, the most correct were the Great Emperors Yao and Shun. They were fortunate to order their lives correctly, and because of that could guide others.

'For proof of the power of this primal strength, take the example of fearlessness – how the heroic spirit of a single valiant soldier can influence an entire army. If a man seeking only renown can produce such an effect, how much more will result from one who rules over Heaven and Earth, keeps all things in the treasury of his intelligence, who simply settles down into his body, whose eyes and ears he knows only provide fleeting images, who knows how to unite all of his knowledge, and whose mind never dies!

'If such a person decided one day to ascend far on high, is there anyone who wouldn't want to follow?

'I only wonder why such a sage is willing to bother with others.'

A Lesson from Below

Taoist Master Po Hun Wu Jen had students from many varied backgrounds, both high-born and low. Among them was Shen Tu Chia, who had lost his feet as punishment for a crime. A newer pupil was Tzu Chan, the Prime Minister of Cheng.

One day when they were sitting together in the hall Tzu Chan turned to the cripple and said, 'I notice that when you see an official you don't get out of the way. Do you think you're equal to a Prime Minister? Now, when I leave the hall first, you must stay behind, and if you go out first, then I'll stay behind. Agreed? I'm now going to leave – will you stay behind, or not?'

Shen Tu Chia replied, 'In our Master's school is there really such a thing as a "Prime Minister"? You take great pride in your official status, and because of it you lord it over others.

'But I have heard that if a mirror is bright, dust doesn't settle on it, and if dust settles on it then it's not really bright. When you study for a long time with someone of virtue, you come to be without error. Over there is our teacher whom you have chosen to make you a better person. But if you still talk like this, aren't you still in error?'

Tzu Chan replied, 'I can't believe a mutilated creature could compare himself to the greatest of emperors! Look at yourself and examine your own virtues! Perhaps you need some self-examination.'

'The cripple replied, 'Most criminals will claim that they were innocent and didn't deserve their punishment. Very few will admit their faults and accept their punishment. But the truly virtuous person resigns himself to the inevitable, and accepts it as his destiny.

'If you stroll in front of a skilled archer's target, his arrow poised to release, that's the spot where you are destined to die. And if you're not hit, that also was destined.

'There are many people with two feet who laugh at me because I lost mine, and that makes me explode with anger. But when I am with our teacher, my anger dissolves, and I return to a calmer mood. I don't know if it's my own aware-ness, or his goodness which washes me of that anger. I have studied with him now for nineteen years, and in all that time I have never been aware of my disability.

'Now you and I are meant to be concerned with our inner selves, yet you are obsessed with my outer body. Aren't you in error?'

Tzu Chan looked uneasy, turned away, and said, 'You won't need to mention this again.'

Toeless Wisdom

In Lu there was a cripple called Shushan the Toeless, who walked on his heels to visit Confucius.

Confucius said to him, 'I see your lack of caution in the past has brought you quite a calamity – isn't it a bit late to come crawling to me?'

Toeless said, 'Through lack of knowledge and taking too little care of my body, I lost my toes. But now I have come to you, still in possession of something more precious than toes, which I'd like to save.

'There is nothing that Heaven doesn't cover, and nothing the Earth doesn't sustain. I assumed that you would be like Heaven and Earth to me – I didn't know that you would receive me like this!'

Confucius was taken aback. 'Forgive me,' he replied. 'Please come inside, where I will try to tell you what I've learned.'

But Toeless stumped out.

Confucius said to his students, 'There's a lesson here! This toeless cripple is still eager to learn how to atone for his past conduct. How much more can be done by those whose virtue is still intact!'

Later, Toeless told Lao Tzu about the meeting. 'Confucius, I think, hasn't yet attained to being a Real Person. Why does he need to keep that crowd of followers around him? He seeks the reputation of being an extraordinary and marvellous sage, and doesn't know that the Real Person considers this to be just so many handcuffs and chains.'

Lao Tzu said, 'Why didn't you make him see the unity of life and death, and that both right and wrong are one category, and so free him from his chains?'

Toeless said, 'Since this is the punishment inflicted on him by Heaven, how can he be freed from it?'

Ugly Body, Beautiful Mind

One day Duke Ai of Lu consulted Confucius:

'I knew of a hideously ugly man called Ai Tai To. People thought so much of him that they always wanted to be by his side. Women said of him, as ugly as he was, "I would rather be one of his concubines than be married to any other man."

'He never took the lead in discussions, but always seemed to share the same opinion as others. He agreed with people but never led them to adopt his views. He only knew what went on in his own neighbourhood.

'He never had a high position, so he wasn't able to help people. He had little money, so he couldn't buy them meals. Yet both men and women flocked to him. He must be a strange character, I thought, so I called him into the palace to have a look. He certainly was ugly enough to scare ghosts!

'But he hadn't stayed with me for more than a month, when I was oddly attracted to the man, and within less than a year I had complete trust in him. Since I had no Prime Minister, I offered the government to him. He responded evasively to my proposal, and looked vague, as if he wanted to decline.

'This made me ashamed and I finally placed the government in his hands. But before I knew it, he left me and went away. I felt crushed, as if I had sustained a great loss, and had no one to enjoy the kingdom with. Tell me, what sort of a man is he?'

Confucius said, 'Once, when I was on a mission, I saw some piglets sucking on their dead mother's nipples. After a while they raised their heads, looked at her, and then ran away, leaving her body. They sensed that she did not see them, and that in some way she was no longer like themselves. What they had loved in their mother was not her body, but what had given *life* to her body.

'Concubines in the royal harem do not trim their nails or pierce their ears: they value the perfection of their bodies. How much greater result could we expect from those who value the perfection of their minds!

'This Ai Tai To, though he didn't speak a word, was trusted by the people. Though he did nothing special for them, they loved him. You appointed him Prime Minister, only afraid that he would refuse. He must have been a man whose inner harmony was perfect, though his realisation of it couldn't be shown by his appearance.'

Duke Ai said, 'What do you mean when you say his inner harmony was perfect?'

Confucius replied, 'Death and life, profit and loss, failure and success, poverty and wealth, superiority and inferiority, blame and praise, hunger and thirst, cold and heat – these are all natural changes of circumstance, the workings of destiny.

'Day and night they succeed one another, but no one knows their origin or what has caused them. We shouldn't let these things disturb our peace or enter our souls.

'The sage radiates harmony and satisfaction, never losing the contentment of his mind, and keeps this state both day and night, so that it's always springtime in his relations with external things. In all his experiences he realizes in his body and mind what's appropriate for each season of the year. These are the qualities of someone whose powers are perfect.'

'And what do you mean by saying that the realisation of these powers couldn't be shown in his person?'

Confucius said, 'Balance is the perfect state of a still lake, and this can serve as a model. Everything within the lake is preserved in peace, and no agitation comes from outside to disturb it. Ai Tai To's virtue was the perfect cultivation of his powers. Even though his inner harmony couldn't be shown because of his ugly physical appearance, people and things couldn't help but be influenced by its powerful force.'

Some days afterwards Duke Ai mentioned this conversation to Confucius' student Min Tzu. 'I used to think it was my work as a sovereign to rule the kingdom, and to pay attention to the lives of the people, only concerned that some might come to a miserable death. This I considered the sum of my duty.

'Now that I've heard the description of a Real Person, I fear my idea is wrong, and that, by wasting my own energy, I may cause the ruin of the state. Confucius and I are no longer ruler and subject, but are soulmates.'

The Beauty Of Ugliness

Yang Tzu told his students about a journey he made, when he spent the night at an inn. The innkeeper had two concubines, one beautiful and the other ugly. Yang Tzu noticed that the ugly one was respected by everyone, while the beautiful one was ignored.

Yang Tzu asked why and was told, 'The beautiful one is so aware of her beauty that we ignore it. The ugly one also realizes how ugly she is, and therefore we don't recognize it.'

Yang Tzu said, 'Remember this, my students. Act virtuously, but don't pride yourselves on your virtue. If you act like this, where can you go that you won't find respect?'

CHAPTER EIGHT

1,001 Uses for the Useless
天

The Useless Tree

Hui Tzu, the Chief Minister of the state of Wei, was Chuang Tzu's best friend, and said to him one day, 'I have a large tree called the Ailantus. Its trunk is so gnarled and bumpy that a carpenter can't apply a measuring line to it. Its branches are so knotted and twisted that the compass and the square can't be used on them. Even though it's planted by the road, no builder bothers to look at it.

'Now this tree is like your words – impressive, but useless. Everyone agrees in ignoring them.'

Chuang Tzu replied, 'Have you ever watched a wildcat or weasel? It lies down, crouching low, until something approaches. Then it leaps and races in every direction, going high and low, until it gets caught in a trap or dies in a net. Or consider the great buffalo, so massive that it's like a cloud darkening the sky. It's so big, yet it can't catch a tiny mouse.

'Now you have a large tree and are troubled because it's useless. Why don't you plant it in a secluded field, or in a wide and barren wilderness? There you could relax idly by its side, or lie down in the enjoyment of untroubled ease, and sleep in its shade. No saw or axe would shorten its existence; nothing can harm it, since it has no use. Why should its use-lessness cause you anxiety?'

Tree of Spirits

Carpenter Shih was on a journey with his apprentice when they came upon an ancient oak tree, which was used as an altar for the spirits of the Earth.

The tree was so broad that it could shelter several thousand cattle. It measured a hundred spans around, and its trunk rose majestically eighty feet above the hill before it threw out its ten branches, each one big enough to be carved into a boat.

So many sightseers came to see this marvel that the atmosphere was like a fair, but carpenter Shih didn't even bother to glance at it, and just went on his way. His apprentice, however, looked long and admiringly at it, and then chased after his master and said, 'Since I've been your apprentice I've never seen such beautiful timber. But you didn't even look at it. Can I ask why?'

'Forget it,' said Shih, 'and don't even mention it. That tree is quite worthless. A boat made from it would sink, a coffin would quickly rot, a piece of furniture would soon fall to pieces, a door would ooze sap, and a beam would be riddled by termites. This tree is good for nothing, and that's the reason it's lived so long.'

That night, when Shih fell asleep, the oak tree appeared to him in a dream and said, 'What other trees are you comparing me to? Are you comparing me to one of those useful trees, fruit trees like cherry, pear, orange, apple, pomelo, lemon and others? But once their fruits ripen they are stripped or thrown down among the dust. Their big branches are broken, and the smaller ones torn off.

'It's because they're useful that their lives are so bitter. They don't complete their natural lives, but are cut off prematurely, and attract the destructive treatment they endure.

'It's the same with all things. I've been trying for a long time to become useless, and twice I was nearly destroyed. But now that I've perfected it, being useless has been of great use to me.

'Suppose I had been useful, could I have grown to this great size? Besides, you and I are both things – how can one thing pass judgement on another? How is it that you, a useless man about to die, can know anything about a useless tree?'

When Shih awoke, he couldn't get this dream out of his head, until his apprentice said, 'If this tree is so useless, how come it stands here as the altar for the spirits of the Earth?'

'Shut up!' was the master's reply. 'Be quiet! It's simply acting as an altar so it can protect itself from harm. If it wasn't used as an altar, it would be in danger of being cut down. It protects and preserves itself in a different way than other things, so to explain it using conventional ideas is a waste of breath!'

Good-For-Nothing

Chuang Tzu was walking in the mountains, when he saw a huge tree with luxuriant foliage. A woodcutter passed by, but he wouldn't touch it, claiming that its wood was of no use for anything. Chuang Tzu said to his students, 'This tree, because its wood is good for nothing, will succeed in living out its natural term of years.'

When he left the mountains, the Master lodged in the house of an old friend, who was glad to see him, and told his son to kill a goose for dinner. The boy said, 'One of our geese can cackle, and the other can't – which of them should I kill?' The host said, 'Kill the one that can't cackle.'

The next day his students confronted Chuang Tzu. 'Yesterday you said the tree would live out its years because of its uselessness, but your friend's goose died because it couldn't cackle – which of these positions, Master, would you prefer to be in?'

Chuang Tzu laughed and said, 'If I said that I would choose a position somewhere between being useful and not being useful, that would seem the right position. But it isn't really, because it wouldn't keep me out of trouble. It's only if I take my position on Tao and its power, and there find my ease and pleasure, that I wouldn't encounter any difficulty.

> 'Out of reach of praise and blame,
> mounting aloft like a dragon,
> descending deep like a snake,
> transforming with the times,
> unwilling to act for my own sake.
> Now high, now low,
> in harmony with everything,
> drifting with the source.

'Treat things as things, but don't let them treat you as a thing. How then can you get involved in trouble?

'Those who define and classify the qualities of things, and teach and practise human relations, don't find life so easy:

> 'Unity brings on separation;
> success breeds ruin;
> sharpness is ground down;
> glory is criticised;
> striving brings stress;
> wisdom is schemed against;
> inferiority is despised.

'Where is the possibility of certainty in all this? Remember this, my students: abide in Tao and its inherent power.'

The Ointment

Hui Tzu told Chuang Tzu one day, 'The King gave me some seeds from a huge gourd, which I planted. The fruit, when fully grown, could contain large quantities of things. I tried to use it to hold water, but it was too heavy to lift. So I cut it in two to make ladles, but the dried shells were too wide and unstable to hold liquid: they were nothing but great useless things! I got so annoyed with them I smashed them to bits!'

Chuang Tzu laughed. 'You are indeed stupid, my friend, in using big things. Let me tell you a story.

'There was once a man from Sung whose family had been bleaching silk for generations. Over time they had developed a formula for an ointment which kept their hands from getting chapped. A stranger heard about this miraculous ointment, and proposed to buy the secret formula for a hundred ounces of gold.

'The family all gathered to consider the proposal. They said, "We've been bleaching silk for generations, and have only made a modest living. Now in one morning we can sell our secret for a hundred ounces of gold – let him have it!" And so the stranger bought the secret formula.

'Later, the stranger went to Wu to give counsel to the King, who was at war with the state of Yueh. The King gave him command of the Navy, and in the cold of winter he fought a sea battle with the enemy's fleet. Before the battle the man gave all his sailors and soldiers the ointment to protect their hands from the icy waters, and they inflicted a decisive defeat on Yueh. The King of Wu was so grateful to the man that he rewarded him with a title and a vast estate.

'The cure for chapped hands was the same in both cases, but the secret was used in different ways. In one case a man got a title, and in the other a man still bleaches silk.

'Now, you had gourds large enough to hold almost anything. Why didn't you think of making large barrels out of them, to let you float down rivers and lakes, instead of giving yourself grief at discovering how useless they were for holding things? Your mind, my friend, seems to be closed against all intelligence.'

Forget the Words

Fishing baskets are for catching fish. But when the fish are caught, you forget the baskets. Snares are for catching hares, but when the hares are trapped, you forget the snares. Words are for conveying ideas. But when the ideas are understood, you forget the words. How I would love to talk with someone who's forgotten all the words!

The Original Technophobe

Tzu Kung was returning home from a journey to Chu when he saw an old man planting his field.

The man had dug a tunnel to reach the water deep in a well, and was now emerging from the tunnel carrying a heavy jar of water to irrigate the field. Sweating and breathing heavily, he expended a great deal of energy, but the result was very small.

Tzu Kung said to him, 'There's a machine that can do this work. With it, a hundred plots of land can be irrigated in one day. With very little energy, the result is great. Wouldn't you like to try it?'

The gardener looked up at him, and said, 'How does it work?'

Tzu Kung said, 'It's a lever made of wood, heavy behind and light in front. By moving it up and down, it raises the water in a constant stream. It's called a well dip.'

The gardener looked angry, then laughed and said, 'I've heard my teacher say that where there are machines, there are sure to be clever minds, and where there are clever minds, there are sure to be scheming hearts.

'When you have a scheming heart in your breast, then your pure simplicity is impaired. When your pure simplicity is impaired, your spirit becomes unsettled, and an unsettled spirit will no longer be a suitable place for Tao.

'It's not that I'm ignorant of this machine, but I would be ashamed to use it.'

Tzu Kung looked blank and felt chastened.

The gardener said, 'Who are you?'

Tzu Kung replied, 'A student of Confucius.'

The gardener said, 'Now I understand. You're someone who studies so that you can become a sage, aiming to impress others with your superiority. You sit alone and sing sad songs, hoping to make a name for yourself. You would make more progress if you forgot your breath and spirit and gave up caring for your body. Since you can't care for yourself, how do you expect to govern the world? Go away and don't disturb my work.'

Tzu Kung shrank back and turned pale. He became disturbed, lost his self-possession, and didn't recover until he had walked quite far.

His students said to him, 'Who was that man? Even since you spoke to him you haven't been your usual self.'

He replied to them, 'Before, I thought there was only one enlightened person in the world, my teacher Confucius, and I didn't know someone like this existed. The Master says that the Tao of the sage is to seek success in his affairs, aim for the true, and use only small amounts of energy to obtain great results.

'Now I see this isn't really so. Those who follow Tao are complete in its powers. Complete in these powers, they're complete in their bodies. Complete in their bodies, they're complete in spirit. To be complete in spirit is the Tao of the sage.

'People like this live close to others, going along with them, but without preconceived ideas of where they're going. Vast and complete is their simplicity! They believe success, gain, cleverness and ingenuity to be a loss of their real mind.

'These people won't go where they don't want to, and won't do what their heart dislikes. If all the world praised them, they would receive it as something best disregarded, and if all the world blamed them, they would see it as losing something accidental and unnecessary. The world's blame and praise give them neither benefit nor injury.

'A person like this can be described as possessing all the powers of Tao, while I can only be called one "tossed by waves and blown by wind".'

When he returned to Lu, he reported his meeting to Confucius who said, 'This man makes a pretence of cultivating the ancient ways. He knows the first thing, but not what follows. He governs what's inside, but not what's outside.

'If you were to meet someone who had become completely unsophisticated, who by doing nothing had returned to his original simplicity, who fulfilled completely his innate nature and embraced his spirit in his arms, enjoying himself by wandering in the world, then you might be surprised!

'But what can you and I learn from the skills of ancient time?'

CHAPTER NINE

The Natural Way

Understanding Life

If you understand the conditions of life you won't strive for what life can't do, and if you understand the conditions of destiny you won't desire to go beyond its reach.

If you want to nourish your body it's necessary to provide food, drink and other material things. But I know cases where more than enough is available, and still the body fails to sustain itself. In order to have life it's necessary to keep it within the body. But I know cases where life hasn't yet left the body, and still the spirit has gone.

> *When life comes,*
> *it can't be avoided.*
> *When it goes,*
> *it can't be stopped.*

It's sad that everyone thinks nourishing the body is enough to preserve life. For when such caring proves insufficient, what in the world can be done that will be sufficient? Though everything we try may turn out to be insufficient, still we feel we ought to try, and don't avoid doing it.

For those who want to avoid caring for the body, the best plan is just to abandon the world.

> *Abandoning the world,*
> *free from entanglements.*

Free from entanglements,
their minds are correct,
and their temperament serene.

Correct and serene,
they secure a renewal of life,
as others have done.
Securing a renewal of life,
Tao is near at hand,
the true secret of their being.

But why is it necessary to abandon the world, and to forget the busyness of life? By renouncing the world's affairs, the body is no longer wearied, and by forgetting the busyness of life, vital energy suffers no loss. When the body is complete and vital energy restored to its original power, we become one with Heaven.

Heaven and Earth are the father and mother of all life. It's through their union that our bodies are formed, and through their separation a new beginning blossoms. When our bodies and vital energy are faultless, we have what I call the transference of power. From vital energy emerges quintessential energy, and we return to assist Heaven.

Doing Nothing Is the Way of the Way

It was the Way of the emperors and kings to regard Heaven and Earth as their parents, Tao and its power as their ruler, and doing nothing as their constant guide.

Doing nothing, non-striving, they used the whole world and still had more left over. Striving, being active, the world used them up and they were drained. This is why the ancients valued doing nothing.

The ancient kings presided over the world, and though

they knew everything about Heaven and Earth, they made no plans. Though their subtle discrimination understood the intricate nature of creation, they did not theorise. Though their power was greater than everything bounded by the seas, they did not act.

> Heaven produces nothing,
> but all things grow and transform.
> The Earth doesn't grow,
> but everything is nourished.
> The emperors and kings did nothing,
> and the world was ordered.

It's said, 'Nothing is more spiritual than Heaven and nothing is richer than Earth. There are none greater than emperors and kings. The inner power of emperors and kings corresponds to that of Heaven and Earth.' This was how they used the actions of Heaven and Earth, carried all life in its course and employed all people in Tao.

The Pure Breath of Life

Lieh Tzu asked gatekeeper Yin a question: 'The Real Person walks under water without drowning, treads on fire without being burned, and soars on high without any fear. How does she do this?'

The gatekeeper replied, 'She does it by guarding her original breath of life and not through any skill or daring. Sit down and let me explain it.

'Whatever has a form, appearance, sound and colour is a thing, and we don't know why one thing is different from another. Why are they all separate? Was one thing created before the others? All we know is that things are just form and colour. But each thing has come from the formless that preceded them all, and will return again to the changeless.

'Now when someone realises this and lives it to the utmost, what can stand in her way and stop her? She will gladly accept her limited place, understanding that it's unlimited. She will lie concealed in the self-knowledge which has no end, will ramble with delight in the beginning and ends of all life. By unifying her nature, by nourishing her vital breath, by concentrating her energy, she will penetrate to the creation of things. In this condition, with her Heavenly qualities whole, and with no flaws in her spirit, how can things get inside and disturb her serenity?

'Take the case of a drunk falling from a carriage: though he may suffer injury, he won't die. His bones and joints are the same as other people's, but the injuries he receives will be different, because his spirit is intact and whole. He wasn't aware of entering the carriage in the first place and didn't know he had fallen out of it. Thoughts of life and death, of danger or fear, don't enter his mind and so he encounters dangers without anxiety. His wholeness has come from alcohol! Imagine what he would be like if his wholeness had come from Heaven!

'Therefore the sage retreats to her Heavenly qualities and nothing harms her.'

Many Transformations, Much Joy

Here is the great force of nature.
I find the support of my body on it.
My life is spent working on it.
My old age seeks ease on it.
At death I find rest in it.
That which makes my life good also makes my death good.

If you hide your boat deep in a ravine, and your net in a

swamp, you imagine that they're safe. But at night a strong man can carry them off, while you in the dark know nothing about it. No matter how well you try to hide little things in larger ones, they will still get away from you.

But if you hide the world in the world, so that nothing could disappear, this is the supreme reality of the ever-constant and enduring Tao.

When a baby is born into her unique form, there is reason for joy. But in life there are 10,000 other forms undergoing incalculable and never ending changes. Shouldn't these also give us endless reasons for joy?

Therefore the sage enjoys herself among things that cannot disappear, and so lives forever. She considers early death or old age, her beginning and end, as equally good, and in this other people imitate her. How much more should they imitate Tao itself, on which all things depend, and from which every change arises!

The Incomplete Sage

Prince Mou, the son of the Marquis of Wei, consulted the thinker Chan Tzu. 'My body is here near the streams and by the sea, but my mind is obsessed with the Royal Court. What advice do you have for me?'

Chan Tzu replied, 'You must set the proper value on your life. If you can do this, profit will seem unimportant.'

The Prince replied, 'I know that, but I can't overcome my desires.'

Chan Tzu replied, 'If you can't control your desires, your spirit won't be satisfied. When you can't control your emotions, but instead try to stop your spirit following them, you do yourself a double injury. People who injure themselves like this are not among the long-lived.'

Mou of Wei was the son of a lord of 10,000 chariots, so

for him to live as a recluse among streams and caves was harder than for a scholar. Although he didn't attain the Tao, we can say he had an idea of it.

Stop Monkeying Around

The King of Wu climbed the Hill of Monkeys and, when the monkeys saw him, they scampered off in terror and hid among the thick hazels. There was one monkey, however, who continued saucily swinging on the branches, completely unconcerned, showing off his cleverness. The King drew his bow and shot an arrow at it, which the monkey nimbly caught, so the King angrily ordered his attendants to rush forward and join the hunt. Thus the monkey was shot and killed.

The King turned and said to his friend Yen Pu I, 'This monkey, by displaying his skill, and trusting in his agility, was arrogant to me. It was this arrogance which brought on its death. Take a lesson from this and curb your haughty arrogance!'

Yen Pu I returned home and became a student of Tung Wu, to eliminate his pride. He put away what he used to enjoy and abandoned all distinction.

After three years the people of the kingdom spoke of him with admiration.

Heavenly Pursuits

Chuang Tzu said, 'To know Tao is easy. It's harder not to speak about it. To know it and not speak about it is to aspire to the Heavenly. To know it and chatter about it is the human way.

'The ancients pursued the Heavenly they found in themselves, and didn't follow their human traits.'

CHAPTER TEN

Confucius

Lessons from the Master

Confucius went west to deposit some books in the Royal Archives of Chou. His student Tzu Lu gave him some advice: 'I understand the former archivist is called Lao Tzu, who has resigned and returned home. If you, Master, want to deposit some books here, why not try to get his help?'

Confucius agreed and went to see the old man, who unfortunately refused to help. Hearing this, Confucius launched into a description of the Twelve Classics to convince him. The old man interrupted him in mid-flow: 'Too many words. Give me a brief account.'

Confucius said, 'They concern Goodness and Justice.'

Lao Tzu said, 'Let me ask if you consider Goodness and Justice to be the essence of human nature.'

'I do,' was the answer. 'If the superior man isn't benevolent and good, he won't fulfil his character. If he's not righteous and just, he might as well not have been born. Goodness and Justice are truly the essential nature of humanity.'

Lao Tzu said, 'Let me ask what you mean by Goodness and Justice.'

Confucius said, 'To be in sympathy in one's inmost heart with all things, to love everyone equally and to allow no selfish thoughts – this is the nature of Goodness and Justice.'

Lao Tzu exclaimed, 'Ah! These are dangerous words! "To love everyone equally!" – isn't that impossible? "To allow no selfish thoughts!" – that is true selfishness! If you really want people to have proper guidance you should imitate the wind in its free movement, and stand firm in your natural integrity! But all this droning on about benevolence and righteousness hurts my brain and disturbs my heart.

'You, Master, should imitate Tao and carry it into practice. If you do this you will reach your perfect end. Why must you keep pushing forward Goodness and Justice, as if you were beating a drum, and searching for a missing child? Ah, Master! You are just confusing people's essential nature!'

Confucius returned home from this interview and didn't speak for three days. His students asked him, 'Master, how did you counsel and correct Lao Tzu?'

Confucius said, 'In him I can say that I've now seen a dragon. The dragon coils itself up, and displays its body. It unfolds itself and reveals its power. It rides on the clouds, and is nourished by Yin and Yang. My mouth hung open, and I couldn't shut it. How could I counsel and correct Lao Tzu?'

Lifting the Lid

Confucius went to see Lao Tzu, and arrived just as the old man finished washing his hair. He was sitting in the sun, his hair spread out, drying. There he sat, completely still and absorbed, as if nothing else in the world existed.

Confucius waited patiently, and then quietly said, 'Are my eyes deceiving me? Is this the real you? Just now, your body seemed as dead as dried wood. You looked as if you had no thoughts at all, as if you had abandoned the world, and were drifting in your own solitude.'

Lao Tzu opened his eyes and replied, 'I was enjoying myself by wandering where all things have their beginning.'

'What do you mean?'

'The mind is too cramped to understand it; the mouth may open but no words emerge to express it. Still I'll try to describe it to you as well as I can.

'The original Yin was cold and austere. The original Yang was fiery and turbulent. Coldness and austerity came from Heaven, fire and turbulence issued from Earth. When Yin and Yang merged, harmony followed and things were born.

'Perhaps something regulated and controlled this, but no one has seen its form. Decay and growth, fullness and emptiness, darkness and light, the changes of the sun and the phases of the moon – this process goes on from day to day, but no one has seen the cause. Life has an origin from which it springs, and death has a place to which it returns. Beginning and end twist and turn together, and no one knows how it ends. If this isn't so, then who is the originator of all this?'

Confucius said, 'Can I ask about the wandering of the mind?'

Lao Tzu replied, 'This wandering is the most precious and pleasant of all occupations. The person who finds this beauty and wanders in such joy we call a Real Person.'

Confucius said, 'Can you tell me how to do this?'

Lao Tzu answered, 'Grass-eating animals don't mind a change of pasture, while creatures born in ponds don't mind if their water is changed. They don't worry about small transformations, but are unwilling to change more important parts of their nature, so joy, anger, sadness and happiness don't enter into their hearts.

'Now, the space between Heaven and Earth is occupied by all things in their unity. When you possess that unity and merge with it, then your four limbs and 100 body parts become just so much dust and dirt. Death and life, your ending and beginning, are merely the succession of day and night, which can't disturb your contentment. How much less will it be troubled by profit and loss, by misfortune and happiness! Those who renounce the trappings of status do it as if they were throwing away so much mud, because they know their true selves are more valuable than any distinctions. The value of your true self can't be affected by a change of status.

'Since numberless transformations will take place before your end is reached, why should any of them trouble your mind? Those who have attained Tao understand this very well.'

Confucius said, 'Master, your virtue is equal to that of Heaven and Earth, but do you still need words to cultivate your inner power? Did the sages of antiquity get beyond this?'

Lao Tzu replied, 'It's not so. Look at this stream, whose water rises and flows – it does nothing, but it naturally acts like this. It's the same with the Real Person and his inner power. He does nothing to cultivate it, yet nothing evades its influence. He's like Heaven, which is naturally high, like earth which is naturally solid, like the sun and moon which naturally shine. Why does he need to cultivate it?'

Confucius reported this conversation to Yen Hui: 'In comprehending Tao I'm like a fly in vinegar. Had the Master not lifted the lid, I'd never have known the sublime unity of Heaven and Earth.'

Making Progress

One day Confucius was talking with his student Yen Hui. Yen Hui said, 'I'm making progress.'

Confucius replied, 'How?'

'I've forgotten Goodness and Justice,' was Yen's reply.

'Very good,' said Confucius, 'but that's not enough.'

Another day Hui again saw Confucius and said, 'I'm

making progress.'

'How?' the Sage replied.

'I've forgotten ceremonies and music.'

'That's also good, but still not enough.'

A third day Hui saw the Master and said, 'I'm making progress.'

'How?'

'I just sit and forget everything.'

Confucius looked startled, and said, 'What do you mean, sit and forget everything?'

Yen Hui smiled blissfully and replied, 'I dissolve all connection with my body and unwrinkle my mind. Freeing myself from my body, and forgetting my knowledge, I inhabit the great void and become one with the Great Presence – Tao. This is what I call sitting and forgetting.'

Confucius said, 'If you're at one with Tao you're free from all discrimination, likes and dislikes. Transformed like this, you've become impermanent. If this is so, then I should become your pupil!'

The Tao of Avoiding Death

Confucius was besieged by his enemies between Chen and Tsai, and for seven days had eaten no hot food.

The Grand Duke Jen went to console him and said, 'You are very close to dying.'

'Yes,' agreed Confucius.

'Do you dislike death?'

'I do,' conceded Confucius.

Jen continued, 'Let me try and explain the Tao that avoids such a death. In the Eastern Sea there is a bird called Yielding. It flips and flops along, floating slowly, flying low, as if it had no power. It takes to the sky only when other birds lead and assist it, and it huddles close to others in the nest.

Yielding is never first in moving forward, and hates to be last at the rear. In eating it doesn't dare take the first bite, but prefers the leftovers. Acting like this, the bird is never alone and exposed, so outsiders, like humans, can't harm it and it escapes injury.

> 'The straight tree is the first to be cut down,
> the well of sweet water is the first to run dry.

'Your aim is to perfect your knowledge and impress the ignorant, to cultivate your character and expose the crudeness of others. A light shines from inside as if you embodied the sun and moon, and this is why you don't escape injuries.
　'I once heard a man of accomplishment say:

> '"Those who boast have no merit.
> Merit that is complete decays.
> Fame that is complete fades."

'Is there anyone who can rid himself of the ideas of merit and fame, and return to the level of an ordinary person?
　'Tao flows everywhere, but the Real Person doesn't dwell in its light. His potential is fulfilled, but he doesn't need to show it. Always simple and ordinary, he appears stupid. Anonymous, he gives up money and power, and doesn't aim at merit and fame. Therefore he doesn't criticise other people and others don't criticise him. The Real Person has no desire to broadcast. Why do you take so much pleasure in it?'
　Declaring 'This is excellent!', Confucius said goodbye to his associates, sent his students home, and withdrew to a wild marshland. There he wore animal skins and hair cloth and ate acorns and chestnuts. He walked among animals without disturbing their herds, and among birds without agitating their flocks. If birds and animals didn't object to him, how much less would people!

Superior Blandness

Confucius was confiding in the recluse Master Sang Hu.

He said, 'I was twice exiled from Lu, a tree was toppled over me in Sung, I had to disappear from Wei, was in extreme poverty in Shang, and was besieged between Chen and Tsai. Besides enduring these calamities, my close associates have gone away, and my followers are deserting me. Why have these things happened to me?'

Master Sang Hu replied, 'Haven't you heard of Lin Hui, the man who fled from Chia? He gave up his jade disc of office, worth 1,000 pieces of gold, and ran away carrying his infant son on his back. People asked, "Did you do this because of money?" But Lin Hui laughed and said a child's value is small compared to a jade disk. Someone else asked, "Was it because of the troubles of your office?" But Lin Hui said raising a young child is more trouble than any job. Why then did he give up the jade token worth 1,000 pieces of gold and rush off with the child on his back?'

Lin Hui explained it. 'The union between me and the jade disc was based on profit. That between me and the child was ordained by Heaven. When the union between people is based on profit, then when pressures of poverty, calamity, distress, and injury come, they abandon one another. When the union is ordained by Heaven, they stick together. How great is the difference between abandoning one another and sticking together! Besides:

> 'Relationships of superior people
> are as bland as water,
> while those of the petty
> are sweet like nectar.

'But the blandness of superior people leads to affection, while the sickly sweetness of the petty leads to revulsion. A union which originates without a strong reason will fall apart for no reason.'

Confucius said, 'I respectfully hear what you say.'

He got up, and strolling slowly and leisurely, totally at ease, he returned home. He put his books away and gave up his studies. Though his students no longer came to bow to him, and be taught, their affection for him increased all the more.

Confucius Finds Tao

Confucius said to Lao Tzu, 'I have studied the Six Classics for a very long time, and know them thoroughly. Even though I discussed them with seventy-two disastrous rulers, and explained to them the Tao of the former kings, not one of them has followed my ideas. It's so difficult to convince people, and to explain Tao!'

Lao Tzu replied, 'I think it's fortunate that you haven't met a ruler willing to adopt your methods! Those Six Classics are just old footprints left by the former kings, but don't tell you how they made those footprints. What you speak about are dried up fossils, and fossils are like footprints – where are the feet that produced them?

'A pair of white herons only need to look at each other without blinking and impregnation takes place. A male insect buzzes in the air above, the female responds below, and impregnation takes place. The hermaphrodite is both male and female and impregnates itself.

'Inner nature can't be altered.
Destiny can't be changed.
Time can't be halted.
Tao can't be blocked.

'If you find Tao, there is nothing it can't do. But if you lose it, there is nothing that can be done.'

After this, Confucius didn't leave his house for three months.

Then he came again to see Lao Tzu, and said, 'Now I understand! Ravens produce their young by brooding, fish by ejecting their eggs, the wasp by transformation. When a new baby is born, the older child cries, knowing it's lost its mother's milk.

'It's been a long time since I played my part in harmony with these transformations, and since I took no part in these natural changes, how could I expect to change other people?'

Lao Tzu said, 'Now you can, Confucius, for you've found Tao!'

CHAPTER ELEVEN

Dealing with Tyrants

Fasting of the Mind

Yen Hui was Confucius' favourite student. One day he came to say goodbye.

'Where are you going?' asked Confucius.

'I'm going to the state of Wei,' said Yen.

'Why?' asked the Master.

Yen replied, 'I hear that the Prince of Wei is immature and rash. He shows little concern about his state, and is blind to his errors. He thinks so little about his people that the dead lie like piles of wood on the plains and marshes. The people don't know where to turn.

'You taught me, "Leave the state that's well governed and go where trouble prevails. At the doctor's door are many sick people." Using your teaching, I would like to devise a plan to cure that state's sickness.'

Confucius said, 'Oh dear! The risk is that you'll become just another casualty. Tao is simple and uniform and doesn't allow complications. When complications are made, the one true path multiplies and leads to confusion. Confusion leads to anxiety, but however anxious you are, you won't be able to save your life.

'The Real People of old first accomplished Tao in themselves, and then offered it to others. If what you have in yourself isn't secure, how can you expect to change a tyrant?

'Do you know how virtue decreases, and knowledge

displays itself? Virtue decreases by pursuing fame, and knowledge displays itself in conflict. Pursuing fame, people fight one another, and knowledge is their weapon. Both of these are destructive, and your conduct should be free of them.

'Now, your virtue is great and your sincerity firm, but you don't understand the spirit of the man you want to influence. Although you're free from any desire for fame, you don't understand his mind. If you try to force on him goodness and justice he'll think you're parading your superiority, and he'll feel abused. One who hurts others is sure to be hurt in return, so you can hardly escape trouble.

'Let's assume that he likes worthy people and hates those who are inferior – then what does he need you for? Before you present your ideas, he, as ruler, will take advantage, and immediately spout his opinions.

'Your eyes will glaze over and you'll be confused. You'll try to look pleased with him and will choose your words carefully. You'll smile submissively, confirming his thoughts. This is like fighting fire with fire, and adding water to floods, increasing the very sickness you deplore.

'Once you give in it will be never-ending. Recognising your failure, you'll be in danger of arguing more stridently, and the end result is sure to be your death. This tyrant only craves fame, power and wealth and just wants more.

'But you must have some idea of how you were going to handle him. Would you like to tell me your method?'

Yen said, 'I will be correct and humble, maintaining single-mindedness and diligence.'

'Oh no!' said Confucius. 'What will that do? You may try to look impressive, but your uncertainty will show on your face, just like any ordinary person. You'll try to read his feelings so you can influence his mind. But he's oblivious to small lessons of virtue, so how will he be moved by your great lessons? He'll be obstinate, and refuse to be influenced. He may pretend to agree with you, but there will be no inner change. How can you act like this and be successful?'

Yen replied, 'Well, while being inwardly firm, I'll outwardly seem to agree with him, and will say that my ideas come from antiquity. Inwardly firm I'll be a follower of Heaven, knowing that the sovereign and I are both children of Heaven. Why would I then be concerned if people praise my words, or not? They'll consider me a simpleton, but I call this being a child of Heaven.

'Outwardly agreeing with the ruler, I'll be friendly to people. Taking part in ceremonies, kneeling and bowing – this is what ministers do. If they can do this, why shouldn't I? Doing what others do, what trouble can I get into? This is what I call being a companion to Humanity.

'I'll declare my ideas and claim their truth as coming from the ancient sages. Although my words may actually condemn the ruler, they'll be those of the sages, and not mine. In this way, though speaking the truth, I'll be free from blame. This is what I call being a follower of antiquity. If I go to Wei acting like this, won't I be successful?'

'No way!' said Confucius. 'How can you succeed like this? You have too many plans, and haven't bothered to analyse them. If you stick to them, you might avoid trouble, but that's as far as it goes. How can they produce the transformation you desire? All this only shows a rigid mind!'

Yen said, 'That's as far as I planned. What method do you think I should use?'

Confucius replied, 'Fasting, and I will tell you about it. But when you have learned this method, will you find it easy to practise? Luminous Heaven will disprove anyone who thinks it's easy.'

Hui said, 'My family is poor. For several months we haven't drunk alcohol, tasted meat or eaten onions and garlic. Is this what you mean by fasting?'

The Master said, 'That's fasting for sacrifice, but not the fast of the heart.

'To fast the heart your heart and mind need to be in perfect unity. Don't listen with your ears, but use the sounding of the heart. Don't even wait for your heart, but listen with your chi, your primal energy. Ears can only listen, the mind can only think, but the chi of primal energy is free from attachment and responsively waits in emptiness. Where Tao abides, there is freedom from attachment, and that emptiness is the fasting of the heart.'

Yen said, 'Before I heard about this, there I was, the Yen that existed. But now if I'm able to use this, the Yen that I was has just passed completely away. Is this what it means to obtain this emptiness?'

The Master replied, 'Entirely. Now you're able to enter this tyrant's cage completely relaxed, and not try to impress him. If he listens to you, let him hear your ideas. If he doesn't listen, be silent. Open no other door, employ no other medicine, but make oneness your home and accept whatever happens. If you do this, you won't be far from success.

'Not to walk is easy, but to walk without touching the ground is difficult. Acting like ordinary people, it's easy to become hypocritical. Acting like Heaven, it's difficult to be false.

'You know about flying with wings but haven't heard of flying without them. You've heard of acting through knowledge but not of acting through not knowing.

'Look at dark empty space. It's in this emptiness that light is born. Harmony arises in a mind stilled like this. When you're not still, your body may be seated but your mind runs around.

'Use the eyes and ears to communicate within, and the knowledge of the mind and heart to penetrate out. When you do this, the spirit will come to you, and how much more will other people!

'This is how all things transform, the secret practice of the great sages of old, and they exercised it all their lives. How much more should we!'

Different Constitutions

When Yen Hui finally went east to the state of Chi, Confucius' face filled with sorrow.

Tzu Kung rose from his mat and approached him. 'Master, why are you so sad at Hui's departure?'

Confucius said, 'That's an excellent question. Kuan Tzu, the Minister of Chi, had a saying that is very true: "A small bag can't contain anything large; a short rope can't draw water from a well."

'It's also true that a person's life has a certain destiny, and his body is adapted in a specific way, so that neither can be added to or subtracted from.

'I'm afraid that Hui will tell the Duke of Chi about the Tao of the great emperors, and relate the words of the sages. The Duke will look within to see if he resembles these sages, and when he finds that he doesn't, will suspect Hui of putting him down. Being suspect, Hui will be killed.

'Have I ever told you this story? One day a seabird landed at the inland capital of Lu. The Earl came out to meet it, brought it to the ancestral temple, and prepared a banquet for it. The sacred music was performed, and an ox, a sheep, and a pig were sacrificed to supply the food. The seabird, however, looked at it indifferently and was miserable. It didn't eat a single thing, nor drink a single sip, and three days later it died.

'The Earl tried to nourish the bird with what he liked, and not with the food the bird needed. To nourish a bird as it should be nourished, let it perch in the deep forests, or roam over sandy plains, or float on rivers and lakes, feeding on eels and small fish, winging with its flock and then resting, being free and at ease.

'It distressed that bird to hear people talk. What did it care for all the noise and hubbub the Earl made about it? If the sacred music were performed at a lake, the animals would run off, birds would fly away and fish would dive to the bottom. But when people hear the sacred music, they gather round and listen. Fish live in water but if people do, they die. They're made differently, and so differ in their needs, their likes and dislikes.

'This is why the ancient sages didn't expect everyone to have the same ability, or deliver the same performance. They applied words according to reality, and gave their approval where they were especially suitable. This was the method of universal adaptation and sure success.'

The Tao of Negotiation

Tzu Kao, the Duke of Sheh, was about to leave on a mission when he decided to consult Confucius.

'The King is sending me on an important mission to Chi. The Prince of Chi will probably treat me with great respect, but will be in no hurry to deal with me. It's difficult enough to hurry an ordinary man, much less a Prince. This worries me no end.

'You have always told me, "Only through following Tao can most things, great or small, be managed successfully. If affairs turn sour, criticism follows, and even if successful, Yin and Yang is disturbed and anxiety can't be avoided. Only the virtuous man, even in the face of failure, can avoid distress."

'My diet is plain and simple, I eat no spicy dishes that make me thirsty. Yet only this morning I received my orders, and this afternoon I'm already gulping iced water. My body's burning up, and the mission hasn't even started! If it fails, I'll be judged harshly. I suffer on two fronts and don't feel capable of carrying out this commission. Can you give me some advice?'

The Master replied, 'In the world there are two great

principles: one is the requirement implanted in our nature and the other is the conviction of what is right.

'The love of a daughter for her parents is implanted in her, and can never be erased from her heart. That a minister should serve his ruler is what is right, and he can't escape this obligation. These are called the great universal principles.

'Therefore a daughter finds peace in serving her parents wherever they may be, and this is the height of devotion. Similarly, a minister finds peace in serving his ruler, whatever the matter, and this is the height of loyalty.

'When you simply obey the commands of your heart, thoughts of sorrow and joy don't arise. There's no alternative to acting as you do, and you accept this as your destiny. This is the perfection of virtue.

'As a minister and a son you must do what can't be avoided. Absorb yourself in your mission and ignore your own self. When will you have time to think of loving life or hating death?

'Act like this and all will be well.

'But let me tell you something else I've learned. If two states are near each other, their mutual trust is proved by actions. If they're far apart, their trust must be conveyed in words transmitted by envoys.

'But conveying messages of satisfaction or dislike is a treacherous job. If both states are happy, the delight is sure to be exaggerated, and if they're unhappy, there will be an excess of annoyance.

'But all exaggeration leads to reckless language, and this distorts the truth. Without truth, distrust arises, and the messenger's life is endangered! That's why the Book of Rules says, "Transmit the message exactly as it stands. Don't transmit it with any excessive language. In this way the envoy can keep himself whole."

'Consider how skilful wrestlers begin with friendly trials

of strength, but always end with underhand attempts to gain victory. As the pressure grows, their moves become wily and clever.

'Those drinking at ceremonies at first observe good order, but always end in disorder. As their excitement grows, etiquette turns into uproar.

'In all things it's the same. People are at first sincere, but always end by becoming unpleasant. At the beginning things are treated as trivial, but as the end draws near, they assume great proportions.

'Words are no different than wind and waves, and actions are a matter of gain and loss. Wind and waves are easily stirred up, and questions of gain and loss easily lead to danger.

'So quarrels are stirred up by nothing so much as clever words and twisted speech, and animosities arise on both sides. When animals are threatened with death, they bellow wildly, and their breath rages angrily. Cornered, they lash out. Similarly, if people are pushed too far, they lash out – why they don't know. Since they don't know why, who knows how it will end?

'That's why the Book of Rules says, "Let the envoy not deviate from his instructions. Let him not press for a settlement." If you go beyond the rules, you'll complicate matters. Departing from instructions and urging on a settlement is dangerous. A good settlement lasts a long time, and a bad settlement can't be altered. Shouldn't you be careful?

'Let your mind be content with the situation you're in. Stay centred, and resign yourself to the inevitable. This is the ultimate you can pursue. What else can you do to fulfil the charge of great Tao? The best thing you can do is also the most difficult – to let things take their natural course.'

Teaching a Tyrant

Yen Ho was about to become tutor to the eldest son of Duke Ling, and he consulted the Minister Chu Po Yu.

'Here,' said Yen Ho, 'is this young man, whose natural disposition is unruly and violent. If I allow him to behave badly, it will endanger the state. But if I try to correct him, my life will be on the line. He has just enough wisdom to recognise the errors of others, but he can't see his own faults. What should I do?'

Chu replied, 'This isn't easy! Be on your guard, be careful, and make sure you keep yourself correct!

'Your best plan is to seek his friendship, and with your mind find harmony with him. But there are dangers connected with both these strategies.

'Stay outwardly close to him, but don't get dragged into his pursuits. Cultivating inner harmony, don't show it. If you take part in his pursuits, you'll fall with him and be ruined, you'll tumble down with a crash. If in maintaining inner harmony, you display it, you'll be noticed, talked about and endangered.

'If he acts like a young boy, then be a boy with him. If you find that he acts unconventionally, you do the same. If you find him reckless, be reckless with him. Understand him so that you can lead him to become free from error.

'Do you know about the praying mantis? It angrily waves its arms in front of speeding carriages, unaware that it has no power to stop them. This shows a high regard for its own abilities. Be on your guard, be careful. If you are too confident of your own abilities, and put yourself in collision with him, you're likely to incur the fate of the mantis.

'Do you know how a keeper of tigers acts? He doesn't dare feed them living animals, for fear of the fury which killing excites. He doesn't even dare to give them whole carcasses, because of the rage which tearing them excites.

Instead he gauges the animals' appetite, understanding their natural ferocity. Tigers are a different species from humans, but they can be trained to be gentle with their keepers, in accordance with their nature. But when a tiger kills a keeper, it's because he's gone against its nature.'

CHAPTER TWELVE

Real People
Real Knowledge

Correcting Nature

Those who want to improve their innate nature through conventional thinking, trying to restore its original condition, and those who want to control their desires by ordinary thinking, seeking to perfect their minds, are deluded and ignorant.

The ancients who found Tao nourished knowledge by calmness and avoided using knowledge to engage in action. Instead they nourished calmness through knowledge. When knowledge and calmness blend and nourish each other, harmony and order emerge from one's inner core. The power of Tao creates harmony, while Tao itself makes it orderly.

When the power of Tao appears in spontaneity and doing nothing, then we have goodness.

When our path is marked by order, then we have true justice and righteousness.

When justice is clearly shown, and all things are regarded with affection, we have compassion.

When people want to improve others, their inner power shrinks, and it can't be extended. If they still try to extend it to others, their original nature will be destroyed.

The Real Knowledge

The perfection of knowledge is to know what Heaven is, and to know what the human is.

What is Heaven? That which gives life. What is human? To know what we truly know and to nourish what we can't know.

The perfection of knowledge is to enjoy one's natural life and not die prematurely.

Although this is so, there's still a problem. This knowledge needs confirmation that it's correct, because it depends on something else. How do we know that what we call Heaven is not really Human? Or that what we call Human is not actually Heaven?

One must first become a Real Person, and then there can be Real Knowledge.

The Real Person

What do I mean by a Real Person?

The Real Person of old didn't rebel against poverty or take pride in riches. He didn't act feverishly to accomplish goals and made no plans to attain them.

Living like this, though he might make mistakes, he had no reason for regret, and though he might have success, he didn't revel in it. Existing like this, he could climb mountains without fear, enter water without being drenched, and go through fire without getting burned. It was through this knowledge that he ascended to Tao.

The Real Person of old slept without dreams, woke without cares, and didn't mind if his food was plain. His breathing was silent and deep, so deep that it came from his heels, while ordinary people breathe from their chest.

When people are defeated, their words come sputtering

out like vomit. Held deep in lusts and desires, their heavenly nature is shallow.

The Real Person of old knew nothing of clinging to life or hating death. Coming into life gave him no joy and he left it without a fuss: calmly he came and calmly he went. He never forgot his beginning, and never wondered what would become of him. He accepted his life and rejoiced in it. He forgot all fear of death and returned to the state before life.

This is what I call not using the human mind to resist Tao, and not using human ways to help Heaven.

This is what I call the Real Person of Tao.

True Goodness

Her mind free from thought,
her appearance calm and tranquil,
her forehead beams simplicity.

Her chill is as elemental as autumn, her warmth that of spring. Her joy and anger flow like the four seasons. She always does what's suitable, and has no limitations. So if a sage has to fight a war and destroy a nation, she won't lose the hearts of the people. Without showing affection her blessings extend through ten generations.

That's why we say that the person who tries to share his happiness isn't a sage, and the person who displays affection isn't benevolent. The one who calculates times and seasons to regulate behaviour isn't wise, and the one who doesn't understand the equality of profit and loss is not a great person. The one who acts for reputation, and loses his natural self, isn't a good student. The person who loses his true self and is without truth can't lead others.

The sages of old all slaved on behalf of others, and tried to give them what they desired, but not by seeking their own pleasure.

The Hidden Power

The Real Person of old appeared unimportant but didn't flatter. Her humility was evident but not servile. Her calmness and contentment gave the appearance of joy, and her radiance drew people's looks. Her blandness concentrated their attention to her virtue. Her quirks were her own, and she wasn't blindly attached to them.

Her every response was from necessity. She accommodated herself to the ways of her generation, but with a certain high-mindedness: her indifference was beyond its influence. Unceasingly she kept her mouth shut, and when she looked down, it was as if she'd forgotten what she wanted to say.

The Real Person of old judged correctly without bias. She considered law to be the substance of government, ceremonies its supporting wings, knowledge to indicate the time for action, and virtue to be in harmony with others.

To consider law the substance of government, one must be flexible. To consider ceremonies as the support, one must guide the people. To consider knowledge as the indicator for action, one must follow the natural course of events. To be virtuous is to be in harmony with others, so she sought with them to ascend its height.

The Real Person of old acted spontaneously, yet the people imagined her accomplishments took immense effort.

She has her likes and dislikes. What she likes is the One and what she dislikes is also the One. What is One is One, and what is not One is also One. When she keeps the One she keeps her Heavenly nature, and in disliking the not One, she accepts her Human nature. When Heaven and the Human are not in conflict, we have Real People.

Forget Yourself in the Tao

Death and life are certain, just like the constant seesaw of night and day – both come from Heaven. We can do nothing about them – that's just how things are.

Some view Heaven as their father, feeling love and reverence. How much more love should they feel for that which stands out superior and alone, the great and most honoured Tao!

Some regard their ruler as so superior that they're willing to die for him. How much more should they do for their True Ruler!

When streams dry up, the fish are stranded on the mud. Rather than wet each other with their dampness, and keep one another moist with their slime, it would be far better for them to ignore one another in the rivers and lakes. Instead of praising and criticising the emperors of old, it would be better to forget all of them, and lose oneself in Tao.

Tranquillity Within Disturbance

Nan Po Tzu Kuei asked the Hunchback Woman, 'You're very old, but your skin is as fresh as a child's. How is that?'

She replied, 'I have studied Tao.'

Nan Po asked, 'Can I learn it?'

She said, 'No, I don't think so! You're not the kind for it!

'There was a man called Pu Liang I who had the talents of a sage, but not Tao, while I had Tao, but not his genius. I decided to teach him to see if he could become a true sage. I thought it would be easy to teach Tao to someone with his abilities.

'So I proceeded, but it was quite difficult.

'After three days, he was able to ignore all worldly thoughts. This accomplished, I worked with him for seven more days, and he was able to transcend all external matters. I carried on working with him, and after nine days more he managed to go beyond his own life. After this, his mind became as clear as morning light, and soon he was able to stand face to face with Tao, able to see the One.

'Seeing the One, he was able to lose all thoughts of past and present. Freed from this, he was able to penetrate to the place where there's no difference between life and death – where the destroyer of life doesn't die, and the creator of life doesn't live. Now he rejected nothing, accepted everything, negated everything, affirmed everything.

'This I call Tranquillity Within Difficulty, meaning that all difficulties only lead to perfection.'

Nan Po asked, 'How did you learn this without a teacher?'

She said,

I learned it from Writing,
who got it from Recitation,
who had it from Clear Understanding.
Clear Understanding got it from Whispered Instruction,
who in turn had it from Daily Use.
Daily Use got it from Great Enjoyment,
Great Enjoyment from Dark Obscurity,
Dark Obscurity from Mysterious Void,
Who heard it from:
The Very Beginning of the Beginning.'

Possessed of Spirit

Chien Wu said to Lien Shu, 'Chieh Yu told some strange and fantastic stories, which related to nothing in reality. I was startled by them – they were as limitless as the Milky Way, incoherent, with no connection to normal experience.'

'What did he say?' asked Lien Shu.

Chien replied, 'These were his words:

'"Far away on Mount Ku lives a man of spirit. His skin is smooth like ice and white as snow. His manners are as shy and delicate as a young girl's. He doesn't eat the fruits of the earth, but inhales the wind and drinks the dew.

'"He ascends on clouds of chi, and drives flying dragons, rambling and enjoying himself beyond the four seas. By concentrating his spirit he protects people from disease and decay, and ensures a plentiful harvest."

'These words seemed wild and incoherent to me, and I didn't believe them.'

'I'm afraid that's the way it really is,' said Lien Shu. 'The blind can't appreciate a drawing, or the deaf a lovely song. But is blindness and deafness only physical? No, there's a similar defect in the intelligence, and of this defect you supply an excellent example.

'That man of spirit, with his powers, embraces all things and rolls them into one. If the age was descending into chaos, and all the people begged him to transform it, why would he bother to take action?

'That man! Nothing can hurt him. The greatest floods, reaching the sky, couldn't drown him. The greatest heat, melting metal and stone, and scorching the ground, he wouldn't feel. From his own energy, he could still mould great leaders like Yao and Shun. Why would he be willing to concern himself with worldly things?'

The Knowledge of the Real Person

Yeh Chueh asked his teacher Wang I, 'Do you know what's common to everything?'

'How could I ever know that?' was Wang I's reply.

Yeh Chueh asked him again, 'Then do you know what

you don't know?' and he got the same reply.

He finally asked a third time, 'Then do all creatures have no knowledge?' and Wang I again said, 'How can I know this, too? Nevertheless, I'll try to say something.

'How can I know that when I say, "I know it", I may really be showing that I don't know it, and when I say "I don't know it", I may really be saying that I do know it?

'Now let me ask you some questions. If someone sleeps in a damp place, he'll have aches and pains, and half his body will feel stiff. But is it the same for an eel? If someone climbs a tree, he'll be frightened and trembling, but is it the same for a monkey? Which of these three knows the right place to live?

'People eat meat, while deer feed on grass. Centipedes like small snakes, while owls and crows delight in mice. Which of these four knows the right taste?

'Monkey mates with monkey, the elk with the doe, while the eel enjoys itself with other fish. You can take the most beautiful woman to the sea, but when the fish see her, they'll dive quickly to the bottom. If she approaches a bird, it'll fly aloft, and if the deer see her they'll scamper away. Which of these four knows the right standard of beauty?

'As I see it, the principles of goodness and justice and the ways of right and wrong are inextricably mingled and confused. How can I possibly know how to discriminate between them?'

Yeh Chueh asked further, 'If you can't discriminate between good and evil, does this mean that the Real Person also lacks this knowledge?'

Wang I replied, 'The Real Person is pure spirit. Lakes might boil around him, but he wouldn't feel the heat. Rivers might freeze, and he wouldn't feel the cold. Thunderbolts might split mountains, and gales shake the sea, without making him afraid. Such a creature mounts on the clouds of the air, rides on the sun and moon, and rambles at ease beyond the four seas. Neither death nor life bothers him, so how much less will he be concerned with good and evil!'

Nameless Advice

Tien Ken, walking south of Mount Yin, came to the River Liao. There he met the Man without a Name, and he put a question to him,

'I would like to ask how to govern the world.'

The Nameless Man said, 'Scram, and take your ignorance with you! Why ask me such a stupid question?

'I am travelling with the Maker of all things. When tired, I mount the bird of ease and emptiness, ride beyond the world, and wander in the region of nowhere, and the wilderness of nothing. Why disturb me with governing the world?'

But Tien Ken persisted with the same question, and the Man without a Name said,

'Let your mind find its pleasure in pure simplicity. Merge yourself with the primordial chi in idle indifference. Let all things take their natural course and allow no personal desire. Do this and the world will be at peace.'

CHAPTER THIRTEEN

Harmonising Differences

The Music of Heaven

Nan Kuo Tzu Chi was sitting leaning against a table. He was staring at Heaven and breathing gently, as if in a trance, unconscious of everything.

His student, Yen Cheng Tzu Yu, interrupted him and said, 'What's going on? Your body looks like dead wood, and your mind like cold ashes. I've never seen you like this before.'

Tzu Chi said, 'Yen, that's a good question. Just now, I had lost myself, do you understand?

'You may have heard the music of man, but you've never heard the music of Earth. And even if you've heard the music of Earth, you haven't heard that of Heaven.'

Yen said, 'Can you describe these to me?'

Tzu Chi replied, 'When the chi of the great mass of nature is aroused, we call it wind. Sometimes it doesn't blow, but when it does, sounds emerge from thousands of openings. Haven't you heard them in a prolonged gale? Take the projecting bluff of a mountain forest: in the great trees, a hundred spans round, there are hollows and openings that look like nostrils, mouths or ears. Sometimes they're square, or round like a bowl, here looking like a footprint and there like a large puddle. The wind rushes in and makes sounds like crashing waves, or whizzing arrows, sharp commands, inhaled breaths, shouts, deep wailing, and a sad moaning.

'The first notes are slight, while those that follow are

deeper, but remain in harmony. Gentle winds produce faint sounds and violent gusts gigantic ones. When the fierce gusts have moved on, all the hollows become empty and still. Haven't you seen this in the swaying and quivering of branches and leaves?'

Yen answered, 'So the music of Earth is simply made by the wind rushing through its openings, and the music of man the sound of flutes, drums and bells. But what about the music of Heaven?'

Tzu Chi said, 'When the wind blows, the various hollows make their own distinct sounds, and when the wind stops the sounds cease, all by themselves. Both of these things arise just from the wind and the openings. Why does anything else need to cause them?'

The Extreme Point of Knowledge

The knowledge of the ancients reached the extreme point. What was that extreme point? In the beginning they didn't know that things existed. This is perfect knowledge, Oneness, to which nothing can be added.

Later, they believed things did exist, but made no distinctions between them.

Then they made distinctions, but expressed no judgements about right or wrong.

It was through making judgements of right and wrong that Tao declined. This injury led to the rise of individual preferences, of likes and dislikes.

Was it really after these preferences arose that the injury came? Or did the injury precede the preferences?

The Still Point of the Mind

If we all followed our true mind, no one would be without a teacher. Not only those of wisdom and knowledge but also the ignorant and foolish.

Not to follow your true mind but still make distinctions between right and wrong is like saying, 'I went to Yueh today, and arrived there yesterday.' It would be making what doesn't exist, exist and what does exist, not exist.

Even the Sage-King Yu, who fought the great floods, couldn't do this, so how can someone like me?

Speech isn't just hot air, since your words have meaning. But if what you say is nonsense, can we say that you're really speaking, or not? You think your words are different than birdsong, but is there really a difference between them?

How has Tao become so obscured that there is a distinction between true and false? How can speech be so obscured that there's right and wrong? Does Tao ever go away? Where can speech not be heard?

Tao is obscured through imperfect understanding and speech is obscured by pretension. That's the cause of arguments between philosophers, one side disputing what the other believes, and vice versa. If we want to decide between them, nothing is better than to focus the clear vision of the Mind of Tao.

All things can be looked at from two points of view: from that and from this. If I look at something from another's point of view, I'm lost. I can only really know it if I know it in myself. Hence it's said, 'That opinion comes from this one, and this opinion from that.' This theory says each opinion gives birth to the other.

Although this may be true, where there's life we find death, and where there's death life also exists. When there's the appropriate there's also the inappropriate. Because there's right there's wrong, and because there's wrong there's right. One can't exist without the other.

So the sage dismisses distinctions, but views things in the light of his Heavenly nature, and through this nature forms a judgement of what's right.

He sees 'this' is the same as 'that', and 'that' is the same as 'this'. 'That' involves both right and wrong and 'this' also involves right and wrong. He doesn't worry about distinguishing opposites, so these opposites merge into the still point of Tao.

When you find this still point, you stand in the centre of the ring of thought, and can respond to endless changes. Right and wrong, this and that, are all just endless changes. Therefore I said 'There is nothing like the clear vision of the Mind of Tao.'

If we were to argue together and you come out on top are you really right and I wrong? And if I get the better of you, am I right and you wrong? Must one of us be right and the other wrong? Or are we both right and wrong? Since we can't see the truth, others will certainly continue in darkness.

Who can I use as referee? If I bring in someone who agrees with you, how can he judge correctly? And the same goes if I use someone who agrees with me. It's no different if I employ someone who either differs or agrees with both of us. Going on in this way, none of us will be able to come to an agreement. Do we have to wait for some great sage?

There's no need for that. Waiting for another to learn about changing opinions is waiting for nothing. We can harmonise conflicting opinions by the invisible operation of Heaven, and by this method complete our years without disturbing our minds.

What do I mean by harmonising conflicting opinions in the invisible operation of Heaven? There's right and wrong and there's Being and Non-being. If right tallies with reality, it's certainly different from wrong, and there's no dispute about that. If being is really being, it's certainly different from Non-being. There can be no dispute about that too.

Forget time. Forget arguments. Let's just appeal to the Infinite, and find our peace there.

Cornucopia

Great Tao cannot be named.
Great argument doesn't need words.
Great goodness isn't good.
Great modesty isn't humble.
Great courage isn't aggressive.

Tao that is displayed isn't real Tao.
Words that dispute don't reach the point.
Goodness always used doesn't work.
Modesty that parades purity isn't genuine.
Courage that's violent must fail.

These five all seem complete, but they tend to become distorted and impaired. Therefore knowing how to stop at what one doesn't know is best.

Who knows the argument that needs no words, and Tao that isn't named? The person who does know has what is called 'The Heavenly Treasure-house'. Pour into it and it's never full, take from it and it's never empty. No one knows why this is so, but we call it 'The Precious Light'.

The Unity of Thought

Tao makes all things.

What is acceptable is acceptable.

What is unacceptable is unacceptable.

We make a path by walking on it.
Things become what we call them.
What are they?
They are what they are!
What aren't they?
They are not what they are not!

Everything has inherent nature and innate capacity. There's nothing which doesn't, and all are acceptable.

Therefore a stalk of grain, a large pillar, a decaying leper and a beautiful woman, the peculiar and the extraordinary, the crafty and the strange, are all alike in the light of Tao.

Their differences are acts of creation.
From creation follows destruction.

But all things, created or destroyed, will again become one. It is only the Real Person who sees this unity. He gives up his own discrimination and follows the ordinary view. The ordinary is founded on the useful. The useful expresses nature, and to realise his true nature leads to happiness. Happiness gained, we are near perfection, and there we stop. We stop, and yet we do not know why. This is Tao.

Three in the Morning

When you exhaust your spirit in the search for unity, without understanding the unity that already underlies things, it's called 'Three in the Morning'.

What is 'Three in the Morning'?

Their keeper was giving the monkeys acorns, and he told them, 'In the morning I'll give you each three and in the evening four.' This made the monkeys angry, so the keeper mollified them, saying, 'All right, all right. In the morning I'll give you four – and in the evening three.' Now the monkeys were very pleased.

The keeper's two proposals were essentially the same, but the first aroused anger and the second happiness.

This is what I'm getting at.

Therefore the sage harmonises both right and wrong, and relies on the natural equality of Heaven. This is called walking both sides of the road.

Clear Vision

My friend the philosopher Hui Tzu, arguing while leaning against a tree, was extraordinary.

His knowledge was nearly perfect. He loved his ideas so much because they were different, and wanted to enlighten others. But since he could never make them clear enough, no matter how much he tried, he ended with obscure discussions about 'the hard' and 'the white'. And his son, too, following his father, accomplished nothing.

If we say that Hui Tzu, acting like this, was successful, then I too am successful. But if he wasn't successful, then neither I nor anyone else has ever been successful.

Therefore the sage is guided by the light emerging from chaos and doubt. He doesn't make distinctions but takes his position on the unchanging. This is called clear vision.

Sense or Nonsense?

I've something to tell you. I don't know whether it's relevant or even interesting. I'm not even sure if this is the right place for it. Although it's not particularly new, it has a character of its own, so I would like to say it.

There is a beginning. If so, there had to be a beginning before that beginning. And there had to have been a beginning previous to that beginning before there was the original beginning.

Then there is Being. There had been Non-being. But was there Non-being before the beginning of that first Non-being? And there must have been Non-being preceding the Non-being before the beginning of Non-being.

If Non-being had suddenly appeared, how would we know if it was really Non-being, rather than Being?

Now I've said something, but I don't know if what I said means something or not.

There's nothing larger than the tip of a hair, and Mount Thai is small. No one lives longer than a baby that dies in its cot, and Methuselah died young.

Heaven, Earth and I were produced together, and all life and I are one. Since we're already one, what else is there to say? But I just said we are one, so speech must also exist.

One plus speech are two, two plus one makes three. Going on from this, the most powerful computer can't reach the end, and how much less can ordinary people!

So if by going from Non-being to Being we arrive at three, how much further can we go if we proceed from Being to Being? No, let's drop that idea, and just stop.

The Miraculous Being of Non-being

Dazzling Light asked Non-being, 'Do you exist, or don't you?'

Getting no reply he looked deeply at Non-being's appearance, which was that of the deepest darkest emptiness. All day long he looked, but could see nothing. He listened hard, but could hear nothing. He grabbed at it, but got hold of nothing.

Finally, Dazzling Light said, 'This is the limit! Who can attain to this? My mind can conceive of ideas of Being and Non-being, but I can't conceive the ideas of the Non-being of Non-being. How does he manage to be the Being of Non-being? Where does he come from to arrive at this?'

The Finest Treasure

If the body is worked hard, without rest, it gets worn out. If the spirit is used ceaselessly, it becomes tired, and when tired, it becomes exhausted.

It's the nature of water, if pure, to be clear, and, if not disturbed, to be level. But when it's blocked and not allowed to flow, it can't preserve its clarity. This is an image of the virtue of Heaven.

> *To be innocent and pure,*
> *to be still and constant,*
> *to be indifferent, doing nothing*
> *is to move and act like Heaven.*

This is the Tao of nourishing spirit.

Now, the owner of the finest sword preserves it carefully in a special box, and doesn't dare to use it, because it's considered a treasure of its kind. But the subtle human spirit radiates everywhere, flowing without limit, reaching to Heaven above and circling round the Earth beneath. It transforms and nourishes all things, and can't be represented by any form.

Its name is 'Supreme Harmony'.

It's only the Tao of pure simplicity which guards and protects the Spirit. When this path is preserved and not lost, it becomes one with the Spirit and this oneness acts in harmony with the order of Heaven.

There's a well-known saying, 'People consider gain to be the most important thing. Pure scholars, fame. The wise and able – ambition. But the sage prizes essential purity.'

Therefore simplicity is that which is not mixed, and purity is that which keeps the spirit whole. Those who embody simplicity and purity we call Real People.

CHAPTER FOURTEEN

The Taoist Teacher

The Time of the Original Chi

Chiang Lu Mien visited his teacher Chi Che with a problem:

'The ruler of Lu asked me to teach him but since I hadn't received instructions from you, I refused. Later I gave in and told him my thoughts. I don't know if I said the right thing, and I'd like you to hear it.

'I told him, "You must be courteous and self-restrained, promote the public-spirited and loyal, and restrain the selfish and servile. If you do this, who wouldn't cooperate with you?"'

Chi Che laughed aloud and said, 'Your words, as a guide for a great emperor, are like the frantic movements the praying mantis makes in trying to stop an advancing carriage – not up to the task.

'Besides, if he followed your advice, he would increase the already dangerous height of his towers and add to the vast number of valuables he collects in them. The people would leave their traditional ways and imitate him.'

Chiang Lu Mien was surprised and said, 'I'm startled by your words, Master, but I'd like you to explain them.'

The Master said, 'If a great sage ruled the kingdom, he would free the minds of the people, help them to carry out his teachings, and change their ways. He would extinguish the greed and aggression in their hearts, and enable them to act in accordance with their innate goodwill. They would assume their own nature did this, and wouldn't realise the sage's responsibility.

'Would such a sage be willing to look up to Yao and Shun as his elder brothers in teaching the people? He would treat these emperors as his juniors, since he himself only wants to maintain virtue and calm stability.'

The Lagging Sheep

Tien Kai Chih was having a discussion with Duke Wei of Chou, who said, 'I understand your Master Chu Hsien has studied life. What has he taught you about it?'

Tien Kai Chih replied, 'When I'm busy sweeping his courtyard, how can I hear my Master's teaching?'

Duke Wei said, 'Don't evade the question, Mr Tien. I'm very interested in what you've learned.'

Kai Chih said, 'I've heard my Master say, "One who skilfully nourishes life is like a shepherd, who rounds up the sheep that lag behind."'

'What did he mean?' asked the Duke.

Kai Chih replied, 'In Lu there was a man named Shan Pao, who lived in the wilderness, and drank only water. He didn't share in anyone's work or the benefits from it. Though he was seventy years old, he still had the complexion of a child. Unfortunately he encountered a fierce tiger, who killed him.

'There was another man called Chang Yi, who spent all his time consorting with the wealthy and powerful, paying his respects. When he was only forty, he came down with a fever and died.

'Of these two men, Shan Pao nourished his inner self, and a tiger attacked his outer, while Chang Yi nourished his outer self, and disease attacked his inner. According to my Master both of them neglected to round up their lagging sheep.'

Confucius said,

'Don't withdraw and hide inside,
don't push forward in display.
Maintain stillness in the centre.
If these three conditions are kept,
fame reaches its greatest height.

'If on a certain road one man in ten is attacked and killed, then everyone warns each other about journeying alone. Isn't this a sign of wisdom?

'But there are serious dangers that ambush people on their couches and beds, and in eating and drinking, but no one knows enough to warn them. Isn't this a sign of error?'

Dozy Wisdom

Old Toothless asked Shabbily-dressed about Tao, and he replied,

'Look after your body,
see it all as one,
and the Harmony of Heaven will come.

Rein in knowledge,
unify consciousness,
and the spirit will reside with you,
the power of Tao will be your beauty,
and Tao will be your dwelling.

Stupid as a new-born calf,
you won't try to understand why.'

When Shabbily-dressed finished speaking, he looked up to find Old Toothless dozing.

He smiled, stood up, and walked away, singing as he went,

'His body like dead wood,
His mind like dead ashes.
Real is his knowledge, solid, true,
no need to ask more questions.
Dim and dark! Obscure!
His mind so empty
no one can consult him.

'What kind of person is this!!??'

The Learned

Chuang Tzu met with Duke Ai of Lu, who told him, 'We have many scholars here in Lu, but very few study your teachings.'

Chuang Tzu replied, 'I disagree. There are very few learned men here.'

'But everywhere in Lu,' replied the Duke, 'you see people wearing scholars' clothing. How can you say there are few?'

'I've heard,' said Chuang Tzu, 'that scholars who wear round caps know the times of Heaven, those with square shoes know Feng Shui, and those who carry semicircular stones deal correctly with all matters.

'But people who really have Tao won't always wear those clothes, so it doesn't follow that those who wear them have Tao. If Your Grace disagrees, why not proclaim that it will be a crime punishable by death to wear scholars' clothing without practising Tao?'

This idea amused the Duke, who issued a decree, and within five days, throughout the entire state of Lu, not one person was seen wearing the clothing of the learned.

But early one morning a very old man was found standing patiently at the Duke's gate – wearing the full kit. The Duke immediately called him in and asked him about affairs of state. Although they talked for days, the Duke found no end to his learning.

Chuang Tzu said, 'When the whole state of Lu can produce only one man who is learned, can we really say there are many?'

The Education of Lieh Tzu

In the state of Cheng there was a mysterious shaman called Chi Hsien. He knew all about people's deaths and births, their gains and losses, their misfortune and happiness, and whether their lives would be long or short – predicting the year, the month and the day like a god. The people of Cheng were terrified of him, and would flee when they saw him coming.

When he was a young man, Lieh Tzu visited the shaman and was fascinated. Returning home, he told his teacher Hu Tzu, 'I used to think your Tao, Master, was perfect, but I've now found something superior.'

Hu Tzu said, 'So far I've only taught you the framework of Tao, and haven't communicated its essence. Do you think you're really in possession of it?

'No matter how many hens there are, without a rooster, they won't be able to lay fertile eggs. You go around displaying your knowledge of Tao to confront the world. You show everything that's on your mind, and this man saw right through you. Bring him here, so that I can see him.'

The next day, Lieh Tzu found the shaman and brought him to visit Hu Tzu. When they came out, the shaman said, 'I'm sorry to say your master is a dead man. He won't survive another ten days! I saw something strange in him – he looked like wet ashes!'

Lieh Tzu wept as he re-entered the house, and as he told Hu Tzu what the man had said, the front of his jacket became drenched with tears. But Hu Tzu remained calm, and said, 'I showed myself to him in the form of the still and silent earth, the calm and immovable mountain. He probably saw me with my hidden power closed up. Bring him to me again tomorrow.'

The next day Lieh Tzu brought him again to see Hu Tzu. When they left, the shaman said, 'It's fortunate for your master that he met me! He's already better: he has all the signs of life! The draining of his vital energy was only temporary.'

Lieh Tzu went in, and reported these words to his master, who said, 'I showed myself to him in the pattern of Heaven, without name or substance on my mind. My vital energy issued from my heels. He saw me releasing my full and natural power. Try to bring him again.'

The next day the two returned, and the shaman saw Hu Tzu. When they walked out, the shaman said, 'Your master is never the same. I can't read his appearance. Let him try to stabilise, and I'll examine him again.'

Lieh Tzu reported this conversation, and Hu Tzu said, 'This time I showed myself in the great harmony of the two elemental forces, in equal balance. He saw my vital energy in its deepest aspect. When water whirls around there is a deep abyss; when still waters gather there is an abyss; when running waters gather, there is an abyss. There are nine different kinds of abyss, and I only showed him three. Try to bring him one last time.'

Next day they came again to see Hu Tzu. They hadn't even sat down, when the shaman lost control of himself and ran out. 'Go after him,' said Hu Tzu, and Lieh Tzu rushed out but couldn't catch up with the terrified shaman. He returned and told Hu Tzu that he had lost him.

Tzu explained, 'I showed myself after the pattern of what existed before I was born. I confronted him with pure emptiness, turning and bending unconscious of anything. Then there was an indistinct swarming which turned and gathered like a tidal wave. This is what made him flee.'

After this, Lieh Tzu realised he had not yet begun to learn. He returned home, and for three years didn't go out. He did the cooking for his wife and fed the pigs as if they were his friends. He took no interest in studies or business. He put away all ideas, and returned to pure simplicity. Rooted in the Earth and centred in his body, amid all of life's distractions he remained one with Tao until the end of his life.

The Foundation

Yi Ir Tzu wanted to become a student of Hsu Yu, who asked, 'What have you learned from your current teacher?'

Ir replied, 'My teacher says, "You must work hard at goodness and justice, and distinguish clearly between right and wrong."'

Hsu Yu replied, 'Why bother to come to me? Since your teacher has branded you with his goodness and justice, and mutilated you with his right and wrong, how will you be able to wander in the Tao of aimless enjoyment, of free and easy contemplation, and enjoy the ever-changing forms of things?'

Ir said, 'That may be, but perhaps I could just skirt its hedges.'

'That's impossible!' said Hsu. 'The blind can't appreciate beauty, or have anything to do with bright colours.'

Ir rejoined, 'But I know when others have lost their strength or wisdom they've regained them by following your system. How do you know that the Maker won't remove the marks of my branding, and restore my mutilation, so that, restored, I can follow you as my teacher?'

Hsu Yu said, 'That we don't know yet, but let me tell you something about it:

'Oh, my Master! Oh, my Master! He gives all things their blended qualities, but doesn't consider himself good. He benefits all generations, but doesn't consider himself kind. He is more ancient than the highest antiquity, but doesn't count himself old. He overspreads Heaven, supports the Earth, and carves and fashions all forms, yet doesn't consider himself skilful.

'I follow him.'

CHAPTER FIFTEEN

The Great Awakening

A Chinese Wake

When his great friend Hui Tzu heard that Chuang Tzu's wife had died, he immediately went to console him. But when he arrived at Chuang Tzu's house he found the sage singing and drumming in front of his wife's coffin.

Hui Tzu was shocked and said, 'When a wife has lived with her husband, raised children, and then dies in old age, not to cry for her is understandable. But isn't it a bit extreme to sing and drum?'

Chuang Tzu said, 'No, it's not. When she first died, it was impossible for me to stay composed and not be affected. But then I reflected on the very beginning of her existence, when she had not yet been born. Not only didn't she have life, but she had no body. Not only didn't she have a body, but she had no breath.

'Because of the intermingling of Yin and Yang, there was a change, and she had breath. Another change, and there was her body. Another change, and there was birth and life. Now there is one further change, and she is dead. The relation between these things is like the cycle of four seasons – from spring to summer, from autumn to winter.

'Now she lies in her coffin, her face pointing to Heaven, and if I were to fall about sobbing and wailing, I would think that I didn't understand what was waiting for us all. I therefore held myself back.'

The Melting Pot

Tzu Szu, Tzu Yu, Tzu Li and Tzu Lai were talking together, when Tzu Szu said, 'Whoever thinks of nothingness as his head, life as his spine, and death as his buttocks; whoever knows how death and birth, consciousness and unconsciousness are one body – he will be my friend.'

The four looked at one other, nodded and smiled, and because they agreed in their hearts, they became friends.

Not long after, Tzu Yu, a crooked hunchback, fell ill, and Tzu Szu went to visit him. 'How great', said the hunchback, 'is the Creator, to have made me so deformed!'

Tzu Yu's internal organs were squeezed into the upper part of his body, and his chin was bent down to his navel. His shoulder was higher than his head, on top of which was a growth pointing to the sky. His breath came and went in gasps. Yet his mind was at ease, and he never complained about his condition.

His visitor asked him, 'Do you dislike being disabled?'

'No. Why dislike it? If the Creator were to transform my left arm into a rooster, I would wait with it for the dawn. If he were to transform my right arm into a crossbow, I would look for a pheasant to shoot and roast. If he were to transform my buttocks into a wheel, and my spirit into a horse, I would ride them, and never need a carriage.

'When we are given our time, we have life in which to spend it. When we lose that at death, then submission is needed. When we rest or submit at the right time, neither joy nor sorrow can affect us.

'This is what the ancients called loosening the cord by which life is suspended. But one who is hung up on things can't loosen himself – he's attached securely by his ropes. That creatures can't overcome Heaven, the inevitable, is a long-acknowledged fact. Why should I dislike my condition?'

Before long another of the friends, Tzu Lai, fell ill, and lay gasping at the point of death, while his wife and children stood around weeping. His friend Tzu Li called on the family, and said to them, 'Please be quiet and get out of the way! Don't disturb his transformation.'

Then, leaning against the door, he said to his dying friend, 'Great indeed is the Maker! What will she now make you into? Where will she take you? Will she make you into a rat's liver, or an insect's arm?'

The dying man replied, 'When a parent tells a child to go east or west, north or south, the child simply follows that command. Yin and Yang are more to a person than his parents. If they bring on my death, and I don't quietly submit, then I am just obstinate.

> 'There is the great Mass of nature.
> I find the support of my body on it.
> My life is spent in labour on it.
> My old age seeks ease on it.
> At death I find rest in it.
> What makes my life good must also make my death good.

'Consider a great founder, casting his metal. If the metal were to leap up in the furnace and say, "I must be made into a sword," the great metalworker would be sure to regard this as uncanny. In the same way, when my new shape is being fashioned in the mould of the womb, if I were to say, "I must become human," the Creator would be sure to regard this as equally strange.

'When we understand that Heaven and Earth are a great melting-pot, and nature like a great foundryman, where can we be sent that won't be right for us?

'We are born as from a quiet sleep, and we die to a calm awakening.'

Mourning

Confucius' student Yen Hui had a question: 'When Meng Sun Tsai's mother died, with all his crying he didn't shed a single tear. In his heart he felt no distress, and during mourning, he showed no sorrow.

'With these three failings people still said he managed the funeral well. Can someone get a reputation with nothing behind it? Frankly, I'm astonished at this!'

Confucius replied, 'Meng Sun is a man who has gone beyond knowledge and found Tao. He has simplified his life, and would have cut out more, but at his mother's funeral he couldn't appear negligent. However, he succeeded in being true to himself.

'Meng Sun doesn't know what purpose life or death serves. He doesn't know which is first and which last. If he's to be changed into something else, he simply awaits the transformation. This is all he does.

'And when we are changing, how do we know that it's taking place? And when we're not changing, how do we know that it hasn't already taken place? Take the example of you and me – are we in a dream from which we have yet to awake?

'Meng Sun looked anguished, but in his heart he wasn't conscious of loss. His mother's death was like her leaving her house at dawn, and not more terrible than that.

'Meng Sun is just more awake than others. When they cried, he also cried, knowing in his heart why he did.

'We all have our own individuality, our "I". But how do we know that this "I" really exists? You can dream that you're a bird, and are soaring in the sky, or that you're a fish, and dive in the deep. But you don't really know whether we two are awake or in a dream.

'Yen Hui, bothering about others is not as good as laughing with them. And laughing isn't as good as letting things be. If you're content with what happens, and just go with it, you'll be able to enter the oneness of mysterious Heaven.'

Burial Plan

Chuang Tzu was dying and his students wanted to give him an impressive burial.

The Master said, 'I'll have Heaven and Earth for my coffin and shroud, the sun and moon for my symbols of jade, the stars and constellations for my pearls and jewels, and all things assisting as mourners. Won't the arrangements for my burial be complete? What can you add to them?'

The students replied, 'We're afraid that the crows and kites will eat your corpse.'

Chuang Tzu said, 'Above ground, the crows and kites will eat me. Below, the worms and ants will eat me. To take from one group and give to the other would mean taking sides.

'If you attempt to produce something even with what is uneven, the result will still be uneven. If you attempt to make the uncertain certain by using what is uncertain, the result will still be uncertainty.

'The person who uses only the vision of his eyes is conditioned purely by what he sees. But it's the intuition of the spirit that perceives reality.

'The wise have known for a long time that what we know through our eyes isn't equal to the intuition of our spirit. Yet most people rely only on what they see, and lose themselves in external things. Isn't this sad?'

Accepting Destiny

Tzu Yu and Tzu Sang were close friends.

Once, when it had rained continuously for ten days, Tzu Yu thought to himself, 'Tzu Sang may be in trouble.'

So he wrapped some rice and went for a visit.

When he came to Tzu Sang's door, he heard a sound something like singing and wailing mixed together. A lute was playing, and he heard the sad words,

> 'Oh Father!
> Oh Mother!
> Oh Heaven!
> Oh People!'

The voice suddenly faltered and the words tumbled out.

Tzu Yu entered and said, 'Why are you singing so sadly?'

Tzu Sang replied, 'I was thinking, and thinking in vain, about how I've come so low. Would my parents have wanted me to be so poor? Heaven shelters everything and the Earth sustains every creature. Have Heaven and Earth singled me out in making me so poor? I was trying to figure out the cause, but I just can't.

'So here I am, on the edge – it must be my fate.'

Borrowed Time

Mr Deformed and Mr One Foot were looking at the graves in the wilderness of Kun Lun, when suddenly a willow tree began to grow from Mr Deformed's left elbow!

Mr Deformed looked at his arm in considerable shock.

Mr One Foot said, 'Do you despise this happening to you?'

'No,' replied Mr Deformed. 'Why should I? Life is just on loan. My body's borrowed, and is just so much dust. Life and death are like the alterations of day and night.

'Just now you and I were looking at the graves of those who've undergone their alteration. If mine is now coming, why should I despise it?'

Bony Thoughts

When Chuang Tzu went to Chu he saw an empty skull, bleached white.

Tapping it, he asked, 'Did you, Sir, die by an axe blow in a war? Or was it through some evil conduct, reflecting disgrace on your family? Or was it because of cold and hunger? Perhaps it was none of these and your time was up?'

That night he took the skull and used it as a pillow. At midnight the skull appeared to him in a dream and said, 'Your words to me were just like an oration. All your talk is about the entanglements of life. After death these don't exist. Would you like me to tell you about death?'

'I would,' said Chuang Tzu in the dream, and the skull continued, 'In death there's no ruler above and subjects below. The changes of the four seasons don't exist, so time flows without end, leaving us tranquil and at ease. No earthly king can be happier.'

Chuang Tzu didn't believe it, and said 'If I could get the Ruler of our Destiny to restore your life, to give you back your bones, flesh and skin, and return your family and friends, wouldn't you want me to do it?'

The skull stared straight at him, knitted its bony brow, and said, 'You're mad! Why should I throw away the greatest happiness and plunge again into the turmoil of human struggle?'

The Spiritual Fire

When Lao Tzu died, Chin Shih went to the funeral, but after yelling out only three times he left.

A student of Lao Tzu said to him, 'Weren't you a friend of the Master?'

'I was,' he replied, and the student said, 'Then is it right to mourn him like this?'

Chin Shih replied, 'It is. I used to think Lao Tzu was the perfect Real Person, but now I don't think so. When I entered and mourned, I saw old men weeping as if they had lost a son, and young men crying as if they had lost their father.

'In attracting and uniting this crowd of followers, there must have been something in Lao Tzu which made them talk about him and cry for him, even though he never asked them to.

'This funeral shows me that Lao Tzu must have suppressed some of his Heavenly nature and permitted an excess of his human feelings – forgetting what he was given at birth.

'This is what the ancients called the crime of neglecting Heaven. When the Master came to earth it was at the correct time. When he died, it was the simple sequence of his life. If we calmly accept what happens at the correct time, and quietly submit to life's changes, this leaves us untouched by grief and joy.

'The ancients described death as the loosening of the cord on which God suspends life. The only thing we can point to is the wood consumed in the fire: this is like our body. But the fire, like our spirit, can be transmitted elsewhere and we can never know where it has gone.'

Standing Apart

Tzu Sang Hu, Meng Tzu Fan and Tzu Chin Chang were drinking and talking together.

One of them said, 'Who can *join* with others without joining with *others*, or *act* together without acting *together*? Who can soar up to Heaven and wander among the clouds, roaming in infinity, forgetting existence?'

The three of them looked at one another and laughed in agreement, becoming good friends.

A short time later, Tzu Sang Hu died suddenly. Before the burial, Confucius heard of the event, and sent his student Tzu Kung to offer assistance.

Tzu Kung found the two remaining friends sitting in front of the corpse, singing a song which one of them had composed, while the other played the lute:

> *'Oh, Sang Hu! Oh, Sang Hu!*
> *Your true self you've got again,*
> *While we, as men, still here remain.'*

Tzu Kung hurried in and said, 'I must ask whether it's according to the rules to sing like this in the presence of the corpse.'

The two men looked at each other and burst into laughter, saying, 'What does this scholar know about ceremony?'

Disturbed, Tzu Kung returned to Confucius and reported the event. 'What sort of men are they? They made none of the usual burial preparations, and treated the body like something alien. They were singing in the presence of the corpse, and their faces registered no sorrow. I can't describe them. What sort of men are they?'

Confucius replied, 'These men occupy and enjoy themselves outside the physical world, while I enjoy and occupy myself within it. There is no common ground for such different people, and I was acting stupidly when I sent you to assist them.

They've become one with the Creator and seek their pleasure in the formless breath of Heaven and Earth. They consider life to be a grotesque tumour, a boil attached to them, and death as just separation from that tumour and a bursting of the boil.

'Holding these views, why should they consider life first and death last? They believe in the theory of the five phases of wood, water, fire, metal and earth, and consider the body organised by them. They ignore their liver and gall bladder, their ears and eyes. They continuously come and go, link ending to beginning, and have no knowledge of start or finish. Careless and clueless, they roam in silent emptiness outside the dust and dirt of the world, and seek their happiness in doing nothing. Why should they bother about the correct ritual, or worry about how they look and sound to ordinary people?'

Tzu Kung said, 'Then why do you, Master, act according to convention?'

Confucius replied, 'I'm condemned by Heaven to live exposed to public view. Nevertheless, I'm willing to share with you what I've learned.

'Fish thrive in water, people develop in Tao. Growing in water, fish gather in ponds, and find nourishment easily. Developing in Tao, people do nothing, and their innate nature is fulfilled.

'That's why it's been said: "Fish ignore one another in the rivers and lakes. People ignore one another in Tao."'

Tzu Kung asked again, 'And what about these people who stand apart from others?'

Confucius replied, 'They stand apart from others, but remain alongside Heaven! So it's said: "An inferior person of Heaven is a superior person on Earth. A superior person on Earth is a small person of Heaven!"'

The Great Awakening

Chu Chiao Tzu and Chang Wu Tzu, two of Confucius' students, were discussing their Master.

Chu said, 'I heard our Master talking about this kind of language: "The sage doesn't occupy himself with worldly things. He doesn't look for profit, or try to avoid loss. He seeks nothing from anyone, and doesn't pursue Tao. He speaks without words and sometimes his words say nothing. He finds his happiness outside the dust and dirt of the world."'

Chu continued, 'The Master considered this kind of language to be a limitless flow of empty words, but I think this describes the mysterious Tao. What do you think?'

Chang replied, 'Words like this would confuse even the Yellow Emperor, so how could Confucius understand them? In any case I think you're too hasty in judging their meaning.

'You see an egg, and immediately look for an omelette. You see a bow and arrow, and immediately look for the roast dove. I'll try to explain it to you in a roundabout way.

'Is there anyone who can stand by the side of the sun and moon, and hold under his arm all space and all time? Is there anyone who can be one with everything, avoid judgements and differences, and ignore fame and power?

'Ordinary people bustle about and strive, but the sage seems stupid and appears to know nothing. He blends 10,000 years together in one conception of time. The myriad things all act spontaneously, and display their power in doing so.

'How do I know that love of life isn't a delusion? And that fear of death may be like someone who's left home, and dreads returning?

'The Lady Li Chi was the beautiful daughter of the Border Guard of Ai. When the Duke of Chin first made her captive, she wept till the tears soaked the front of her dress. But when she came to the Duke's palace, shared his luxurious bed, and ate his delicious food, then she wondered why she had wept.

'How do I know that the dead don't repent their former craving for life?

'Those who dream of feasting may cry and moan in the morning, while those who dream of grief and sorrow may wake to go out hunting. When they were dreaming they didn't know it was a dream and in their dream they may even have tried to interpret it. But when they awoke they knew that it was a dream.

'One day there will be a great awakening, after which we will know that life itself is a great dream. In the meantime, the stupid believe they are already awake, and think they know things, calling one man ruler, and another servant.

'How foolish! You and Confucius are both dreaming. I, who say that you are both dreaming, am dreaming myself. These words may seem very strange, but after 10,000 ages we'll meet a great sage who knows how to explain it all. Who knows? We might find him unexpectedly at any time.'

The Dream

Shade said to Shadow, 'Before you were walking ahead, and now you've stopped. Before you were sitting, and now you've stood up. Why are you so undecided?'

Shadow replied, 'These actions are mine all right, but I have no idea how I do them. With the sun and light I make my appearance, and with darkness and night I fade away. I'm dependent on another before I exist, and that other in turn depends on something else. When it comes, I come with it, and when it goes, I go with it. How can I know why I do one thing, or don't do another?

'Once I, Chuang Tzu, dreamt that I was a butterfly, a

colourful butterfly floating along on the air, feeling happy
and carefree. I didn't know that I was Chuang Tzu. Suddenly
I awoke, and was myself again, this same Chuang Tzu.

'Now, I don't know if I was Chuang Tzu dreaming that I
was a butterfly, or if it was a butterfly dreaming that it was
Chuang Tzu. But between me and the butterfly there must be
a difference, and it is this separation that is called "the transformation of things".'

CHAPTER SIXTEEN

The Seeker

1. The Reluctant Sage

Among the students of Lao Tzu there was one, Keng Sang Chu, who understood some of his Master's teaching, and wanted to put it into practice with his followers in the north, at the hill of Wei Lei.

Students he judged pretentious know-it-alls he sent away, and concubines who were overly kind he kept at a distance. He decided to live only with those who were off-hand and rude, and employed only the rough and ill-mannered.

After three years there were great harvests in Wei Lei, and the people remarked, 'When Master Keng Sang first came here, we were alarmed by his strangeness. We thought he couldn't do us any good, but now we've known him for three years, his presence is extremely beneficial. Surely he must be a sage? Why don't we revere him as the representative of our departed ancestors, and build an altar to him as our god of the earth and grain?'

Keng Sang heard about this and was unhappy. His students thought this odd, but he said to them, 'Why do you think this strange? When spring's breath arrives, vegetation grows; when autumn arrives, fruits of the earth ripen. Do spring and autumn do this without a cause? It's just the processes of Great Tao in operation.

'I was taught that the Real Person keeps calm deep within his house, while the people rush around, unthinking and crazy, not knowing what they are doing.

'Now these petty people of Wei Lei want to present their offerings to me and place me among the wise men. But should I be set up as a model? This is what makes me unhappy, especially when I think of the teaching of my Master.'

His students said, 'You mustn't think like this. In a ditch eight yards wide, a big fish can't turn around, but minnows and eels find it very congenial. On a small hill a large animal can't hide, but foxes find it excellent cover. Besides, the wise should be honoured and the able rewarded, while preference should be shown to the good and beneficial. The ancient Emperors Yao and Shun acted like this. How much more should the people of Wei Lei do so! Please, Master, indulge them!'

Keng Sang replied, 'Come nearer, my children, and listen. Suppose there was an animal so big that it could grab a carriage in its mouth. If it left the hills, it wouldn't escape the danger of being trapped in a net. Or if a whale that could swallow a boat was left stranded on the shore, then even ants would be able to bother it. That's why birds and animals aim to be as high as possible, and fish and turtles dive as deep as possible. In the same way a person who wants to preserve his body and life keeps concealed, and does so in the remotest place possible.

'Besides, what did those Emperors do to deserve your praise? In their arguments it was as though they recklessly tore down walls to plant wormwood and brambles in their place, or thinned their hair before combing it, or counted the grains of rice before cooking. They did everything with finicky discrimination, but how did that help the world?

'If you promote the talented, you create disorder, making the people compete with one another. If you employ the wise, the people steal each other's reputation. Those who calculate life can't make the people good and honest. Indeed, the people are very eager for gain – a son will kill his father, and a minister his ruler for it. People steal in broad daylight, and at midday tunnel through walls. I tell you the root of this great disorder was planted in the times of Yao and Shun. The branches of it will remain for a thousand ages, and after a thousand ages people will surely be found eating one another.'

2. The Perplexed Student

Nan Jung Chu was an older student and seeker of Tao, and he asked Keng Sang Chu, 'What means can an old man like me adopt to become a Real Person?'

Master Keng Sang said,

'Keep your body intact,
hold on to your vital energy,
don't let your thoughts be turbulent.

'Do this for three years, and you may become a Real Person.'

Nan Jung replied, 'Eyes are all formed the same, there's no difference between them, but the blind can't see. Ears are all the same, no difference between them, but the deaf can't hear. Minds all have the same nature, no difference between them, but the insane can't use theirs.

'My body and mind are like yours but somehow there is a gap between us. I'd like to find myself, but I'm not able to do it. You've now said to me,

'Keep your body intact,
hold on to your vital energy,
don't let your thoughts be turbulent.'

'With all my efforts to learn Tao, your words go no further than my ears.'

Keng Sang replied, 'There is nothing more I can teach you.'

'There is a saying, "Small flies can't transform the bean caterpillar; fowls from Yueh can't hatch geese eggs, but fowls from Lu can." It's not that the power of these fowls is different, but their ability or inability comes from the differences of big and small. My ability is small and isn't sufficient to transform you. Why don't you go south to see Lao Tzu?'

3. The Three Dilemmas of Nan Jung Chu

Nan Jung Chu prepared some food, and walked seven days and nights, arriving alone at the house of Lao Tzu.

The Master said to him, 'Have you come from Keng Sang Chu?'

'I have,' said Nan Jung.

'Why have you brought this crowd with you?'

Nan Jung was surprised, and swung his head round to look behind. Lao Tzu said, 'Don't you understand my meaning? You've come here with your mind stuffed full of ideas and problems, instead of coming here empty.'

Nan Jung lowered his head and sighed, then lifted it up and said, 'I didn't understand your question, and I've now forgotten my own question.'

'What do you mean?' asked the Old Master.

'I have a predicament. If I'm not wise, people say I'm stupid, and if I'm knowledgeable, this disturbs my body. If I'm not good, then I harm others, while if I am good, I cause myself distress. If I'm not just, I'm accused of injuring others, while if I am just I upset myself.

'These three dilemmas bother me and I walked here to seek your advice.'

Lao Tzu replied, 'When I first looked into your eyes, I understood you, and your speech confirms my judgement.

You look bewildered and confused, as if you've lost your parents, and are using a pole to try to find them at the bottom of the ocean. You've gone astray and are at your wits' end. You want to restore your original nature, but don't know how to do it. You're in a sorry state!'

4. First Teaching: Close the Gates

Nan Jung Chu entered Lao Tzu's school and the Master suggested he try to develop the things he liked, and dismiss all unpleasant thoughts.

For ten days he meditated and fasted, then went again to Lao Tzu, who said to him, 'Even though you're purifying yourself, you still seem anguished. You're still clinging to things you dislike.

'When external influences trouble you, you'll find it very difficult to try and control them. Better to stop their invasion by protecting your inner core. Likewise, when internal impulses bother you, it's difficult to hold them in check. Better to close the gates of your self against their leaving. A master of the Tao wouldn't be able to control these two influences acting together, and how much less can one who is only a student!'

5. Second Teaching: Thaw the Ice

Nan Jung Chu said, 'A villager fell ill, and when his neighbours asked about it, he was able to describe the symptoms, even though it was an illness he hadn't had before. When I ask you about Grand Tao, it's like taking medicine which only increases my sickness. It's enough for me if you can just explain the Tao of keeping good health.'

Lao Tzu replied, 'You ask about keeping good health.

'Can you embrace the One?
Can you keep from losing it?
Can you know good and bad fortune without consulting the
*   oracle?*
Can you rest where you ought to rest?
Can you stop when you have enough?

'Can you leave others alone and seek it in yourself alone?
Can you flee from desire?
Can you be sincere?

'Can you become like a little child? A child can cry all day without becoming hoarse – so perfect is its harmony. It can clench its fists all day without relaxing its grip – such is the concentration of its power. It can stare all day without moving its eyes – so unconcerned is it by the outside world. It walks but doesn't know where. It rests where it's placed, but doesn't know why. It unconsciously mingles with things, and just follows their flow. This is how to guard life.'

Nan Jung Chu said, 'And are these the characteristics of a Real Person?'

Lao Tzu replied, 'No. This is called thawing the ice, and melting the frost.

'Can you do it?

'The Real Person, along with others, shares food from Earth, and happiness from Heaven. But unlike others, he doesn't relate to considerations of profit and loss. Unlike others, he doesn't do strange things, form plans, or have projects. He flees the allure of desire, and pursues his way with complete simplicity.

'This is the way he guards his life.'

'And does this constitute perfection?' asked Nan Jung Chu.

'Not quite,' said Lao Tzu. 'I will ask again whether you can become like a little child, a newborn who acts without knowing what it's doing, and walks without knowing where it's going. Its body is like dried-out wood, and its mind like cold wet ashes. Because of this, good and bad fortune don't affect it. Experiencing neither good nor bad fortune, how can it suffer human calamities?

'When your mind reaches such spontaneity, it emits a Heavenly light, and in this light everything is revealed: people reveal their humanity and things their substance. When a person has cultivated himself to this point, he becomes constant. When he is constant, others will seek refuge with him, and Heaven will help him. Those in whom others take refuge we call the People of Heaven. Those whom Heaven helps we call the Children of Heaven.

'Those who seek this by study look for something that can't be learned. Those who seek it by effort, attempt what effort can never achieve. Those who seek it by reason, use reason where reason has no place. Knowledge of when to stop when you can't arrive by knowledge is perfection. Those who can't grasp this will be destroyed by Heaven.'

6. Third Teaching: Maintain Inner Sincerity

Lao Tzu continued, 'When everything is done to maintain the body; when the mind is aware of possible dangers; when inner reverence is cherished and given freely to others; if all this is done, and bad fortune still arrives, it's due to Heaven, and not to humanity.

'These misfortunes will not be enough to disturb your serenity, or to invade the Spirit Tower of your heart and mind. This Tower has a Guardian but unless you know this Guardian he won't recognise you.

'If you try to accomplish anything without this inner sincerity, every attempt will fail. Malign influences will enter, and you will be unable to free yourself from them. Every fresh attempt will bring still greater failure. If you do evil in daylight, people will punish you. If evil is done in darkness and secrecy, the spirits will inflict punishment. Understand your relations both to people and spirits, and then you'll know what to do in the solitude of yourself.'

7. Fourth Teaching: Preserve Inner Freedom

One who preserves his inner self doesn't act for the sake of fame. One who lives for the world has his will set on whatever he can take. One who acts without thinking of fame may seem ordinary, but shines brightly. One whose will is set on gain is just a trader.

People see how he stands on tiptoe, while he thinks he's naturally superior. A person attached to things becomes possessed by them, while one indifferent to things just lets them pass by.

Attached to things, you lose concern for other people. Unconcerned with others, everyone becomes a stranger. In this way a person becomes alienated from others.

There is no weapon deadlier than the will – even the sharpest sword is inferior to it. There is no robber greater than Yin and Yang, from whom nothing escapes. But it's not Yin and Yang that do the robbing – it's your own heart that does it.

8. Fifth Teaching: Hide in Non-Existence

Tao is in everything, found in the complete and the divided. To divide something is to create something else. To create something is to destroy something else.

So when people emerge and are born, if they don't know how to return to their previous non-existence, they are little more than ghosts. Everything that is born also returns – or dies, as we say. They may be killed off and gone, but their life is like that of ghosts.

If the formed can learn from the unformed, then true understanding can take place. We emerge, but not from a root. We return, but not through an opening. We have a real existence, but it's not located in a place. We have duration, but it has nothing to do with beginning or end.

We have a real existence, but it has nothing to do with place: that's our relation to space. We have duration, but it has nothing to do with beginning or end: that's our relation to time.

We have life, we have death; we emerge, we return. To emerge and return without showing our form is called the 'Gate of Heaven'. The Gate of Heaven is Non-being.

All forms of life come from Non-being. The first beings couldn't bring themselves into Being – they must have come from Non-being. And Non-being is just the same as Non-existing.

So the sage hides himself in Non-existence and this is his great secret.'

9. Sixth Teaching: Find Real Knowledge

Lao Tzu continued his teaching: 'Among the ancients there were those whose knowledge reached the extreme point. What was that point? There were some who thought that in the beginning there must have been nothing. This was the extreme point, the furthest reach of their knowledge, to which nothing could be added.

'Next were some who supposed that in the beginning there was existence, and they considered life to be a gradual ebbing, and death a return to the original state. There they stopped, but they made a division between life and death.

'Then there were those who said, "In the beginning there was nothing. Later there was life. And in a while life was succeeded by death. We believe that Non-existence is the head, life the body, and death the buttocks. Anyone who understands that Existence and Non-existence, death and life, are all under One keeper, will be our friends."

'Although these three views are different, they belong to the same family. They are one, even though they seem to be diverse.'

10. Seventh Teaching: All Life Is One

Lao Tzu continued: 'The possession of life is like dirt collected under a cooker. When this is distributed in different forms, we consider it different. But to try to talk about these differences is a waste of breath. There is always something we don't understand.

'For instance, at the Winter Sacrifice the intestines and hooves of the sacrificial animal are placed on separate dishes, but we don't consider them parts of different victims. The animal is one.

'Again, when you inspect a house to buy, you go over all of it in detail – bedrooms, shrines and toilets – making estimates of different parts of the house. But the house is one.

'Let me speak about how people make distinctions. Life is the root, and knowledge is applied to it. Using knowledge, people examine life, and debate right and wrong, trying to determine what will bring them fame and fortune. Their conclusion is that only they know what's right, and they try to make others adopt them as a model, even prepared to die to defend their views.

'These people believe being an official is a mark of knowledge, and not being in office a sign of stupidity. They think success entitles them to fame, and failure is a disgrace. The people of the present day who follow this method are like the cicada and the little dove – there's little difference between them.

'If you tread on someone's foot in the crowd, you apologize. If an older brother steps on his younger brother, he comforts him. If a parent treads on a child's foot, no need to ask forgiveness.

'Hence it's said:

'"Perfect politeness shows no special respect;
perfect justice takes no account of things;
perfect wisdom makes no plans;
perfect good shows no emotion;
perfect loyalty gives no oath of sincerity."'

11. Eighth Teaching: Keep a Calm and Stable Mind

Lao Tzu concluded his teaching to Nan Jung Chu,

'Suppress the impulses of the will;
unravel the errors of the mind;
untie the knots of virtue;
unblock the free flow of Tao.

'Glory and riches,
prominence and position,
fame and profit;
these six are the impulses of the will.

'Personal appearance and style,
beauty and cleverness,
excitement and memory;
these six are errors of the mind.

'Hatred and desire,
pleasure and anger,
sadness and joy;
these six are the knots of virtue.

'Rejection and acceptance,
receiving and giving,
knowledge and ability;
these six obstruct the free flow of Tao.

'When these four conditions
and their six causes
no longer disturb your heart,
then you will be correct.

'Being correct, you are calm;
being calm, you are clear;
being clear, you are empty;
empty –
the state of doing nothing,
in which everything gets done.

'Tao is revered by all the virtues.
Life is when their power can shine.
Nature is the substance of life.

'Nature's movement we call action.
When action is false,
it fails to strike home.

'People who are knowing attach themselves to things outside and always have a plan. With all their knowledge there's always something they miss – they can't see straight.

'When you act because there is no alternative, it's called "virtue". When you act from your deepest self, it's called "governing".

'You may think these two terms are opposed to each other, but in reality they are in agreement.'

So ended the Master's teaching.
Did Nan Jung Chu ever find Tao?
Did he keep his health and guard his life?
We shall never know.

*Further information on Taoism
can be obtained from:*

The British Taoist Association
16 Birch View
Epping CM16 6JT

Tel: 01279 832325
Secretary: Peter Smith

Web Site: *www.Taoists.co.uk*